GRAMSCI'S POLITICAL THOUGHT

Gramsci's Political Thought

An Introduction

ROGER SIMON

LAWRENCE AND WISHART
LONDON

Lawrence and Wishart Ltd
39 Museum Street
London WC1A 1LQ

First published 1982
© Roger Simon, 1982

Printed and bound in Great Britain at
The Camelot Press Ltd, Southampton

Contents

Acknowledgements

This book has greatly benefited from comments by Sam Aaronovitch, Noreen Branson, Pat Devine, Betty Matthews, George Matthews and Jeff Skelley. The responsibility for the contents is of course mine.

1 Introduction

Britain and Marxism

Since the war the position of Britain in the world has
undergone far-reaching changes. The ending of the British
Empire exposed the economy to the full force of competition
from the other advanced capitalist countries and revealed the
long-standing weaknesses of British manufacturing industry.
Thus when world capitalism entered into a period of deep
crisis in the 1970s Britain was affected with particular force. A
variety of important political developments have been taking
place. Among ruling circles there has been doubt and
uncertainty as to the future and a search for new approaches,
reflected in the sharp shift to the right inside the Conservative
Party and in the birth of the Social Democratic Party.

In these conditions it might have been expected that the
labour movement would gather much greater popular
support. But it has also been facing grave difficulties.
Certainly the trade union movement has become much
stronger than it was before the war, through the growth of the
shop stewards organisation and a great expansion of
membership among white collar workers and in the public
sector. But there has not been a comparable development of
the political struggle for socialism. From the high point
reached in 1945-51 there was a gradual decline in electoral
support for the Labour Party; its share of the vote in 1979 was
37 per cent compared with nearly 49 per cent in 1951. It is
true that a very important process of renewal has been taking
place since 1979 inside the Labour Party. But a powerful
broad movement consciously supporting socialist policies, and
capturing the imagination of wide sections of the population

including the youth, has not yet developed in Britain. The labour movement has built up great defensive strength. But it has yet to achieve hegemony (national leadership) in the sense in which Gramsci uses this term and which it is one of the objects of this book to explain.

Considering the depth of the crisis affecting British capitalism, Marxism as an organized political force does not exert as much influence as might have been expected. An organised Marxist movement has a long tradition in Britain, stretching back to the foundation of the Social Democratic Federation in 1883, and was greatly strengthened by the foundation of the Communist Party in 1920, which has played a significant part in a great many spheres of national life, particularly in the trade union movement, ever since, and has sustained a daily newspaper since 1930.

However the size of the Communist Party has declined since the end of the Second World War and this decline was not arrested by the remarkable growth of interest in Marxism which developed in the late 1960s. These years witnessed a spread of radical movements and ideas on an international scale, especially in the United States and Western Europe, reaching its highest point in the dramatic events in France in May 1968. In Britain, there was the movement against the war in Vietnam, the growing militancy in the trade unions, the upsurge of the students' movement in universities and colleges, and the new wave of feminism, re-creating the women's movement – as Women's Liberation – in an entirely new and deeply influential form; there was also the ecology movement and a great variety of community movements.

The rise of these social movements was accompanied by a great expansion of the influence of Marxist ideas. Members of the Labour Party, the Communist Party, and of the various parties associated with Trotsky's thought such as the International Socialists (later the Socialist Workers' Party) and the International Marxist Group, were active in all the new movements and played an important part in the spread of Marxism, which however, mainly took the form of a tremendous expansion in the publication of books and journals about Marxism, and in the teaching of Marxism in universities and colleges. In this form, Marxism can therefore be said to have established for itself a very significant place in British society. Even so, its influence has not yet spread widely so as to affect the lives and outlook of the mass of the people. It is not yet a major social force in Britain.

It is possible to draw attention to a number of factors affecting Britain which help to explain this situation, such as the special characteristics of the British labour movement. But it is not the purpose of this book to examine all of these. Here I want to consider one factor, namely, that Marxist theory has from the beginning suffered from a major defect: *economism*. This has prevented an adequate understanding of the nature of capitalist domination, and of the strategy required to end that domination and advance to socialism.

While economism was subjected to a powerful criticism by Lenin, there were important limitations in his approach. It was the Italian Marxist Gramsci who showed, by his work in developing his concept of *hegemony*, how these limitations of Leninism could be overcome, and how the full potentiality of Lenin's critique of economism could be realised. In order to understand Gramsci's work, therefore, it is necessary to begin by considering the nature of economism.

In examining this, I assume that the reader already possesses a basic knowledge of Marxism, acquired by studying some of the writings of Marx, Engels and Lenin.

Economism

Economism can be defined as the interpretation of Marxism which holds that political developments are the expression of economic developments; the line of causation proceeds from the economy to politics which tends to be deprived of any autonomy of its own. One form of economism is the view that history possesses a necessary movement, independent of the human will, derived from the continual growth of the productive forces. Capitalism is seen as developing inexorably towards economic crisis and collapse as the contradiction between the forces and the relations of production become greater. An economistic approach is reflected in the widespread use of the metaphor 'base and superstructure' which is derived from Marx's famous preface to the *Contribution to a Critique of Political Economy* (1859). The significant developments are understood to be those taking place in the economic base, whereas political struggles are considered only part of the superstructure erected on the base.

This kind of 'mechanical determinism', as Gramsci called it, was very influential among some of the socialist parties adhering to the Second International in the years before the First World War, among which the German Social Democratic Party was the most prominent. In Gramsci's view, mechanical determinism tended to promote a passive attitude of waiting for the inevitable economic collapse and this discouraged the exercise of political initiatives by the labour movement. This could leave the movement helpless in face of a political crisis, and was one of the causes of the collapse of the parties of the Second International in 1914.

Gramsci considered that an economistic outlook also lay at the root of the failure of the Italian Socialist Party to give the kind of leadership required in the revolutionary upsurge of 1919-20, and which resulted in its suicidal passivity in face of the subsequent rise of fascism. Because of their economistic outlook, the Italian Socialist leaders did not consider that revolution would arise from a shift in the balance of class forces brought about by a series of political initiatives. Rather, it was believed that, as the contradictions of capitalism grew, the necessary mass movement would spontaneously arise and sweep the socialist party into power. Thus the Italian Socialist leaders made no serious attempt to build up a broad alliance around the working class composed of the new social forces arising among the peasants and the urban petty bourgeoisie; instead, they allowed these forces to be mobilised by Mussolini's Fascist Party, leaving the labour movement isolated and ensuring a popular basis for the ultimate triumph of fascism.

Economism has proved to be extraordinarily persistent and

deep-rooted in its various manifestations, and nowhere is this more true than in Britain, as is shown by the contrast between the remarkable strength of the trade union struggles for better wages and conditions, and the relative weakness of the political struggle for socialism. The limitations of a *trade union consciousness*, which Lenin criticised in Russia in 1902, have been very evident in our country.

Lenin criticised a particular form of economism in his writings against certain trends in the movement at the beginning of the century, in particular in *What is to be done?* (1902). His attack was directed against various Russian groups and their newspapers, such as *Rabochaya Misl* (Workers' Thought). They claimed that the economic (trade union) struggle around wages and conditions of work was the 'most important, the most widely applicable' means of arousing the political activity of the workers; the movement should concentrate on the economic struggle, and the workers would spontaneously develop socialist consciousness out of their trade union struggles. Lenin argued, on the contrary, that the trade union struggle could only develop trade union consciousness, and that in order to develop political consciousness the workers had to take up the struggle against the oppression of the Tsarist autocracy as it affected all other social classes, strata and groups of the population, in all aspects of their lives and activities, religious, scientific and cultural. In *Two Tactics of Social Democracy* (1905) he opposed the Mensheviks for accepting the political leadership of the Russian capitalists in the struggle against Tsarism. The Menshevik strategy would leave the Russian labour movement in what he called a 'guild' or 'corporatist' phase, limited to trade-union struggles in defence of sectional interests. By contrast, Lenin argues that the working class should move beyond the corporatist phase and should, in alliance with the peasantry, act as the leading (hegemonic) force in the democratic struggles against Tsarism.[1]*

Later on in 1917 the revolution triumphed when the

* See page 133 for notes and references.

Russian working class, under the leadership of the Bolsheviks, succeeded in combining the class struggles against the capitalists with a range of massive democratic movements – of the peasantry for the land, of the workers, peasants and soldiers against the war, and of the oppressed nationalities for their freedom. The working class emerged as the national leader of all these democratic struggles. Since Lenin developed in practice and in theory the concept of leadership by the working class of a broad alliance of social forces, Gramsci regarded him as the founder of the concept of hegemony (SPN 381).

Limitations of Marxism-Leninism

Lenin's achievements can perhaps be summed up by saying that, in his writings as well as in his political practice, he stood for the primacy of politics. If it is accepted that capitalism does not contain within itself some essential quality which propels it towards inevitable collapse, it follows that the outcome of any economic crisis depends on the conscious actions of human forces, that is, on political interventions.

However, it is essential to distinguish between Lenin's political practice and his writings as they related to the working-class movement in Russia, and the body of theoretical principles which were taken over and developed by the Communist Parties of the Third International (the Comintern) after Lenin's death. These principles, which have become known as Marxism-Leninism, contained serious limitations, and remained in important respects within an economistic framework. It is not possible to make a full analysis of these limitations without unduly prolonging this chapter.[2] Instead, they will be examined at relevant points in the course of explaining the concept of hegemony. But one limitation of particular importance will be examined at this stage.

As mentioned above, the Russian working class gained political power in 1917 because it succeeded, under Bolshevik leadership, in combining the massive popular struggles of the

Russian people and of the oppressed nationalities with the class struggle of the workers against the capitalists. Thus Lenin clearly perceived the importance of social conflicts which developed during the war and which could not be reduced to conflicts at the level of the relations of production. However, this perception was limited to a revolutionary situation. Marxism-Leninism did not succeed in working out an adequate theory of the link between class struggles and these popular-democratic conflicts in non-revolutionary periods, when capitalism was relatively stable. Thus the primacy of the political was reserved for revolutionary situations; in periods of stability there was a tendency to revert to an economistic approach.

One illustration of this was the difficulty which the Comintern and the Communist Parties in Western Europe had in coming to terms with social democracy in the 1920s after the postwar revolutionary upsurge had subsided.[3] The Comintern at first adopted a policy of striving for a united front with social-democratic parties. However, confronted with the temporary stabilisation of world capitalism, its hostility towards these parties grew stronger, and early in 1928 it adopted an extremely sectarian approach, presenting social-democratic governments and fascism as two different forms of bourgeois dictatorship, and eventually characterising social-democratic leaders as 'social fascists'. Thus the complexity of social democracy, with its right and left wing tendencies, was simplified and presented in purely class terms; it was seen as the main obstacle to the advance of the revolutionary movement. The international Communist movement was deeply imbued with a form of economism consisting in the reduction of popular movements and struggles to purely class struggles, and which has since become known by the rather clumsy term of *class reductionism*.

In the early and mid-1920s the British Communist Party achieved considerable success, in pursuit of the united front policy, in building an alliance with the left in the trade unions (the National Minority Movement), with the left in the Labour Party (the Left Wing Movement) and with the unemployed (the National Unemployed Workers Movement). However, this aroused the intense hostility of the TUC and Labour Party leaders. By a series of bans and proscriptions Communists were excluded from the Labour Party and were prevented from holding office in a number of trade unions. It was this fierce attack, and the right-wing policies pursued by Macdonald, Bevin, Citrine and others, that led the British Communist Party, after a prolonged debate, to accept the Comintern's policy at its 1929 congress. Its slogan in the general election that year was 'class against class'[4]; for the next three years it pursued an extremely sectarian policy, abandoning all its previous efforts to work with the Labour and trade union left and cutting itself off from other working-class organisations.

The rise of Hitler's fascism in 1933 transformed the political situation. Fascism and the danger of war became the main threat to social advance. Dimitrov's report to the Seventh Congress of the Comintern in 1935 proposed that Communist Parties should take the lead in building a broad anti-fascist people's front based on the united front of the working class in alliance with the peasantry and petty bourgeoisie. In practice this meant striving for unity between communists and social democrats, and parties representing other sections threatened by fascism's destruction of civil liberties and parliamentary democracy. This policy had considerable success, especially in Spain and France where popular front governments were formed. In Britain the membership and influence of the Communist Party, which had declined during the 'class against class' period, grew quite rapidly, mainly as a result of the party's activities in the struggle against fascism and the war danger and, perhaps above all, its wholehearted defence of the inspiring struggle of the Spanish Republic against Franco.

Yet the political practice of the Communist parties was now in advance of the Marxist-Leninist theory about democracy. In Lenin's booklet *State and Revolution* (1917), one of the most influential of all his works and a central reference point for subsequent Marxist discussions about the state, he defines the state as 'an instrument of the ruling class', and as a 'machine for the repression of one class by another'. It follows that parliamentary democracy under capitalism is only democracy for the ruling class; it is a dictatorship over the working class. In a socialist revolution it is necessary for the proletariat to destroy the parliamentary democratic state and replace it by a fundamentally different type of state, soviet democracy, which will be the dictatorship of the proletariat over the capitalists. Thus Lenin assumes that there is a mechanical relation between economics and politics – between changes in the economic structure and changes in the form of the state. For capitalism the appropriate form of state is a parliamentary democracy; for socialism it is a system of direct democracy based on soviets.

Lenin wrote *State and Revolution*, and other works expressing the same views, in 1917-18 when the Russian working class was mobilised around the soviets, whereas the opposing classes were grouping around the Constituent Assembly (a form of parliamentary democracy) which was dissolved by the Soviet Government early in 1918. His approach at this particular period was not the same as that taken by Marx and Engels at earlier periods, or indeed as his own views at other stages of the movement in Russia. But his writings on the state in 1917-18 became an integral part of the orthodoxy of Marxism-Leninism after his death.

The Marxist-Leninist theory of parliamentary democracy was a serious handicap for the Communist parties engaged in the struggle for popular fronts. If parliamentary regimes were instruments of bourgeois domination to be swept away in a socialist revolution, Communists were open to the criticism that their defence of parliamentary democracy was only tactical; alternatively, the Communists were permanently committed to parliamentary democracy, in which case it could not be a pure expression of capitalist domination. This contradiction was partially resolved in the new programme adopted by the British Communist Party in 1951, *The British Road to Socialism*, which declared in favour of a parliamentary road to working-class power rather than a soviet road; the parliamentary state was to be transformed into a socialist parliamentary state, instead of being replaced by a soviet type of state.

But this solution, while it was a major step forward, still left the theoretical issue of the nature of democracy, and the relation between socialism and democracy, unsolved. Gramsci's concept of hegemony provided the solution, based on the recognition that popular democratic struggles, and the parliamentary institutions which they have helped to shape, do not have a necessary class character. Rather, they are a terrain for political struggle between the two major classes – the working class and the capitalist class. In order to advance to socialism, the labour movement has to find the way to link these popular democratic struggles with its socialist objectives, building an alliance which will enable it to achieve a position of national leadership (hegemony). The great achievement of Gramsci was to elaborate this conception of hegemony which had been pioneered by Lenin. The struggle for a broad democratic alliance forms the central theme of the revised version of the Communist Party's programme, *The British Road to Socialism*, adopted at its 1977 congress. But to overcome the limitations of economism in the British labour movement, far more than the adoption of a programme is necessary. What is required is the transformation of the way of conducting politics – of the political practices – of the labour movement.

The theme of this book is that a widespread understanding of Gramsci's concept of hegemony is an essential part of this process of transformation.

The Prison Notebooks

The story of Gramsci's life, from his birth in 1891 in the Sardinian town of Ales until his death in 1937 after ten years in Mussolini's prisons, has been movingly told by Giuseppe Fiori[5]; and the principal events in his life are set out at the end of this book. His first experience of the leadership of a mass movement was gained when he edited the weekly journal *L'Ordine Nuovo* ('The New Order') which helped to inspire the great factory councils' movement in Turin in 1919-20. His ten years of intense political activity culminated in 1924-26 when he was general secretary of the Italian Communist Party. During these two years the influence of the ultra-left in the party, mainly due to its first general secretary Bordiga, was largely overcome and the great majority of the party was won over to Leninist principles as Gramsci understood them. His active political life was ended by his arrest in November 1926. The Prison Notebooks were written between 1929 and 1935. In spite of the extraordinarily difficult conditions, the lack of any Marxist classics which he had to quote from memory, and his bad health which became steadily worse under the harsh prison regime and the lack of medical attention, he succeeded in filling 2,848 closely packed pages in 33 notebooks. In 1935 illness prevented him from writing any more, and he died on 27 April 1937, three days after his release from prison.

He is considered by Italian Communists to have been the leading figure in the foundation of their party, because of his practical activities as a political leader, and through the inspiration of his thought as set down in his Prison Notebooks. The Notebooks were not published in Italy until 1948-51 (in six volumes); but an invaluable continuity was provided through the leadership of his outstanding colleague Palmiro Togliatti, who was a member of the *L'Ordine Nuovo* group with Gramsci in 1919-20, and leader of the Italian Communist Party from the time of Gramsci's arrest until his death in 1964.

Gramsci was a polemical thinker, for his thought was stimulated through criticising and commenting on the ideas of others. So his notebooks are filled with critical comments, ranging in length from a few lines to several pages, on articles and books, past and contemporary (for he was able to get some contemporary Italian journals and books in prison), on Italian and European intellectuals and on historical events. From 1933, when his health deteriorated rather sharply, he began to rearrange some of his notes into longer series on the same subject; examples are the notes on Machiavelli's Politics entitled 'The Modern Prince', and the notes on Italian history. Yet the Notebooks remain essentially fragments never intended for publication, and many of the most important concepts which Gramsci develops are not defined with any precision. More than once he insists on the provisional, tentative character of his notes; many of the statements are only a 'first approximation', and some of them might be abandoned as a result of further research, and even the opposite might turn out to be more correct. (Q 438 and 935).

This tentative, undogmatic approach is one of Gramsci's most attractive characteristics. But it has the consequence that, in spite of the coherence of his thought, it is not at all easy, in reading through the Notebooks, to grasp the full significance of his contribution to Marxism. The aim of this little book is to provide an introduction to Gramsci's political thought as set down in his Prison Notebooks and earlier writings. Any attempt at a simplified presentation of his ideas is bound to lose a great deal of the flavour and richness of his writing; there can be no substitute for reading the Prison Notebooks. At the same time any introduction, however simple, is bound to involve interpretation of his thought. This is necessary because of its tentative and provisional character; and also because there have been great political, economic and social developments in Italy, Britain and other capitalist countries since Gramsci was writing. There were inevitably limitations in Gramsci's thought, just as there were in Lenin's, and some of these are examined in this book. A very important contribution to the development of Gramsci's ideas has been made by the Italian Communist Party, especially by Togliatti but also by many other Marxist thinkers. An immense literature has grown up around Gramsci in Italy, and a small selection of this has now become available in English translation. Some valuable contributions have been made by Marxist writers in Britain to the development of his ideas and their application to our own history and recent political developments. I have tried to take into account everything which is available in English. This element of interpretation must therefore be born in mind by the reader. The next chapter gives a preliminary outline of Gramsci's concept of hegemony and of the other concepts which are related to it.

2 Gramsci's Concept of Hegemony: an outline

1. *Coercion and consent.* The starting-point for Gramsci's concept of hegemony is that a class and its representatives exercise power over subordinate classes by means of a combination of coercion and persuasion. In his notes on Machiavelli's *Prince*, Gramsci evokes the mythical Greek centaur, half animal and half human, as a symbol of the 'dual perspective' in political action – the levels of force and consent, authority and hegemony, violence and civilisation. Hegemony is a relation, not of domination by means of force, but of consent by means of political and ideological leadership. It is the organisation of consent. In some passages in the Prison Notebooks, Gramsci uses the word *direzione* (leadership, direction) inter-changeably with *egemonia* (hegemony) and in contrast to *dominazione* (domination). The use of the term hegemony in the Gramscian sense must be distinguished from the original Greek meaning, the predominance of one nation over another. (There are, however, a few passages in the Prison Notebooks where Gramsci uses hegemony in its ordinary sense of predominance to refer to relations between nations or between town and country).

2. *The Leninist foundation.* The foundations of the concept of hegemony were laid by Lenin who built on the work which had been done by the pioneers of the Russian Labour movement. As Perry Anderson has shown, the term hegemony was first used by Plekhanov and other Russian Marxists in the 1880s to denote the need for the working class to lead an alliance with the peasantry for the overthrow of Tsarism.[6] The working class should develop a national approach, fighting for

the liberation of all oppressed classes and groups. This was developed by Lenin, as we saw in the previous chapter: the Russian working class should, in alliance with the peasantry, act as the leading (hegemonic) force in the bourgeois-democratic revolution for the overthrow of the Tsarist autocracy. In this way the working class, then a small minority of the population, would be able to win the support of the great majority of the people.

3. *Hegemony becomes a concept.* For Lenin, hegemony was a strategy for revolution, a strategy which the working class and its representatives should adopt to win the support of the great majority. Gramsci adds a new dimension to this by extending it to include the practices of a capitalist class or its representatives, both in gaining state power, and in maintaining that power once it has been achieved. The first note on Italian history, written in the first of the 29 Prison Notebooks, is headed 'Class political leadership before and after attaining governmental power'. Gramsci distinguished between domination (coercion) and 'intellectual and moral leadership':

> A social group can, indeed must, already exercise 'leadership' before winning governmental power (this is indeed one of the principal conditions for the winning of such power); it subsequently becomes dominant when it exercises power, but even if it holds it firmly in its grasp, it must continue to 'lead' as well (SPN 57-68).[7]

Thus Gramsci transforms hegemony from a strategy (as in Lenin) into a concept which, like the Marxist concepts of forces and relations of production, of classes and of the state, is a tool for understanding society in order to change it. He developed the idea of leadership and its exercise as a condition for achieving state power into his concept of hegemony. Hegemony is a relation between classes and other social forces. A hegemonic class, or part of a class, is one which gains the consent of other classes and social forces through creating and maintaining a system of alliances by means of political and ideological struggle. The concept of hegemony is constructed with the aid of a number of other concepts which are related to it. That is why any short definition of hegemony is inadequate. I will now give a brief outline of these concepts, which will be discussed in more detail in later chapters.

4. *The relations of forces: economic corporate/hegemonic.* The notion of building up a system of alliances is central to the concept of hegemony. In 'Some Aspects of the Southern Question', the notes he was writing at the time of his arrest, Gramsci said:

> The proletariat can become the leading and the dominant class to the extent that it succeeds in creating a system of alliances which allows it to mobilise the majority of the population against capitalism and the bourgeois state (SPW II 443).

The working class can only develop into a hegemonic class by taking into account the interests of other classes and social forces and finding ways of combining them with its own interests. It has to go beyond sectional, or what Gramsci calls *economic-corporate* struggles, and be prepared to make compromises, in order to become the national representative of a broad bloc of social forces. Thus the relation between the two fundamental classes of capital and labour is not a simple one of opposition between two classes only, but is a complex one involving other classes and social forces. Each side strives to strengthen its own pattern of alliances, to disorganise the alliances of the other, and to shift the balance of forces in its favour.

5. *National-popular.* For Lenin, hegemony was conceived mainly in terms of an alliance of classes or parts of classes. Gramsci adds a very important new dimension with his concept of *national-popular:* a class cannot achieve national leadership, and become hegemonic, if it confines itself only to class interests; it must take into account the popular and democratic demands and struggles of the people which do not have a purely class character, that is, which do not arise directly out of the relations of production. Examples are the

radical and popular struggles for civil liberties, movements for national liberation, the women's movement, the peace movement, and movements expressing the demands of ethnic minorities, of young people or of students. They all have their own specific qualities and cannot be reduced to class struggles even though they are related to them. Thus hegemony has a national-popular dimension as well as a class dimension. It requires the unification of a variety of different social forces into a broad democratic alliance expressing a national-popular collective will, such that each of these forces preserves its own autonomy and makes its own contribution in the advance towards socialism. It is this strategy of building up a broad bloc of varied social forces, unified by a common conception of the world, that Gramsci called a *war of position*.

6. *Passive revolution* In analysing the war of position carried on by the two fundamental classes for hegemony, Gramsci draws a basic distinction between the strategy employed by the capitalist class and that which is appropriate for the working class. The strategy of the bourgeoisie has a special quality which he called *passive revolution*. He developed this concept out of his analysis of the Risorgimento, the movement for the unification of Italy in the mid-nineteenth century. Although there were a number of popular uprisings in the course of the Risorgimento, the national unification of Italy (involving the expulsion of the Austrians) and the accompanying rise to power of the capitalists in Northern Italy, was achieved mainly through the agency of the state of Piedmont, its army and monarchy, instead of mobilising the majority of the population by supporting the demands of the peasants for agrarian reform. Thus the Risorgimento was a 'revolution from above', made in the main through the agency of the Piedmontese state: a passive revolution.

Gramsci suggests that a strategy of passive revolution is the characteristic response of the bourgeoisie whenever its hegemony is seriously threatened and a process of extensive reorganisation is needed in order to re-establish its hegemony. A passive revolution is involved whenever relatively far-reaching modifications are made to a country's social and economic structure from above, through the agency of the state, and without relying on the active participation of the people. Social reforms which have been demanded by the opposing forces may be carried out, but in such a way as to disorganise these forces and damp down any popular struggles. It follows that the appropriate strategy for the working class is an *anti-passive revolution* founded on the continual extension of class and popular-democratic struggles (see paragraph 11 below on the *war of position*).

7. *Intellectual and moral reform*. For the working class, the task of passing from the economic-corporate phase to the hegemonic phase requires a transformation in the political consciousness of the working class and also of the members of other classes and groups whose support is needed for the broad alliance. Ideology acts as the cement or cohesive force which binds together a bloc of diverse classes and social forces. The cementing ideology cannot therefore be a pure class ideology, expressing only the class interests of the capitalist or working class. It has to be a synthesis, taking into account the unique historical traditions of any country and the contributions made by the diverse social movements which make up the hegemonic bloc. This process of ideological struggle was called by Gramsci *intellectual and moral reform*.

This requires an understanding of the nature of ideology and of the way in which peoples' ideas are related to their practical activities. Gramsci insists on the materiality of ideology, namely, that it has a material existence in the social practices of individuals. Ideologies are not individual fancies, rather, they are embodied in communal modes of living and acting. In order to understand the relation between an ideology and the individuals who are influenced by it Gramsci starts with what he calls *common sense*, the uncritical and largely unconscious way in which a person perceives the world, often confused and contradictory, and compounded of folklore, myths and popular experience. (He is of course giving the term a special meaning, quite different from the usual one, somewhat akin to the English terms 'conventional wisdom' or 'received opinion'.) The task for Marxism is to be a criticism of common sense, and to enable people to develop its positive nucleus – which he called good sense – into a more coherent outlook.

8. *Civil society*. We have been analysing different aspects of the relations of forces – the contrast between economic-corporate and hegemonic, the importance of national-popular struggles and the nature of ideological struggle. Capitalist society is understood as a complex network of relations between classes and other social forces, dominated by the struggle between the two fundamental classes, capital and labour. These social relations are embodied in a great variety of organisations and institutions including churches, political parties, trade unions, the mass media, cultural and voluntary associations. One set of institutions, the apparatuses which make up the state, are separated from all the rest in having a monopoly of coercion. All these social relations and the organisations which embody them (other than the state with its coercion) are called by Gramsci *civil society*. The social relations which make up civil society are distinct from the relations of production, and the organisations within civil society are distinct from the apparatuses which make up the state. (The nature of this distinction is explored in chapter 9.) Civil society is the sphere of class struggles and of popular democratic struggles. Thus it is the sphere where hegemony is exercised.

9. *Historic bloc*. A class which is advancing towards hegemony in civil society must also achieve leadership in the sphere of production. It is only because the bourgeoisie acquires a decisive control over the productive process that it can also become the hegemonic class in civil society and achieve state power. But the control of the capitalists over production has never been absolute; it has always been contested by the workers, and there have been struggles by them and their trade unions over the conditions of work and over the terms for the introduction of new machines. The metaphor of base and superstructure is therefore unsatisfactory. It is misleading to think in terms of a sharp separation between a sphere of economics (production of

surplus value) and a sphere of politics (struggle for state power). On the contrary, the social relations of civil society interpenetrate with the relations of production. Although the Prison Notebooks contain many references to base and superstructure, the direction of Gramsci's thought, and his rejection of economism, is against it. Instead, he uses the term *historic bloc* to indicate the way in which a hegemonic class combines the leadership of a bloc of social forces in civil society with its leadership in the sphere of production. Stated briefly, the notion of historic bloc may not seem very clear; it is discussed more concretely in chapter 10 on the factory councils' movement of 1919-20.

10. *The nature of power.* Marxism-Leninism has tended to take the view that power is concentrated in the state, and that the aim of revolutionary strategy is the capture of power (symbolised by the storming of the Winter Palace in 1917). Only *after* the capture of power by the working class can the construction of socialism begin.

Gramsci suggests that power is best understood as a relation. The social relations of civil society are also relations of power, so that power is diffused throughout civil society as well as being embodied in the coercive apparatuses of the state. Gramsci used the term *integral* state to describe this new conception of the nature of power, which he summed up as 'hegemony armoured by coercion'. It follows that the political struggle of the working class for socialism cannot be confined to the winning of state power, but has to be extended to the whole of civil society. It is necessary to win a substantial measure of hegemony in civil society as a condition for gaining control over the state. The achievement of control over the state is only part (though a decisive part) of the transition to socialism.

11. *War of position.* In one of the best-known passages in the Prison Notebooks Gramsci compared civil society to a powerful system of 'fortresses and earthworks' standing behind the state. And he drew a comparison between Tsarist Russia and the West:

In Russia the state was everything, civil society was primordial and gelatinous; in the West, there was a proper relation between state and civil society, and when the state trembled a sturdy structure of civil society was at once revealed (SPN 238).

Thus power was highly concentrated in the state in Tsarist Russia and the capture of power in a single historical moment was possible. But in countries where civil society is well developed, as in Western Europe, a 'war of movement' has to give way to a different strategy, a 'war of position'. Revolution is a process of expanding the hegemony of the working class – of the building up of a new historic bloc – and is not a sharp rupture at a single moment when state power passes from one class to another. Thus the transition to socialism consists of two distinct processes, interacting with one another: the growth of working class hegemony, and the transformation of the state into a socialist state.

Perhaps even this brief outline of the concept of hegemony and the associated concepts is enough to convey the far-reaching character of Gramsci's contribution to Marxist political theory. The concept of civil society as the sphere of class and popular-democratic struggles, and of the contest for hegemony between the two fundamental classes, adds a new dimension to Marxism. It develops very significantly the Marxist theory of political power and of the revolutionary process.

3 The Relations of Forces

Transcending the corporate phase

A subordinate class can only become a hegemonic class by developing the capacity to win the support of other classes and social forces. It has to learn to go beyond sectional or corporate activities, when it is concerned only with its own immediate interests, and advance towards the hegemonic phase by taking into account the interests of other classes and groups as well. The relation between two fundamental classes, feudal and capitalist, or capitalist and working class, has never been a simple one of opposition between two classes only, but a complex network of relations involving other classes, groups and social forces.

Gramsci's principal note on the relations of forces (SPN 180-83) is one of the key passages in the Prison Notebooks. He begins with the proposition that the level of development of the material forces of production provides the basis for the emergence of the various social classes, each one of which has a specific position within production itself.

So far Gramsci is simply giving the classical Marxist definition of the emergence of a class. His distinctive contribution comes with his analysis of the relation of political forces. He takes the rise of the capitalist class as his example, and distinguishes between three phases in the development of collective political consciousness and organisation. The first two of these are *economic-corporate* (often shortened to *corporate*) while the third is *hegemonic*.

1. The first and most elementary phase is when a tradesman feels obliged to stand by another tradesman, a manufacturer by another manufacturer, etc., but the

tradesman does not yet feel solidarity with the manufacturer. The members of a professional group are conscious of their common interests and of the need to organise, but are not yet aware of the need to associate with other groups in the same class.

2. The second and more advanced phase is that in which consciousness is reached of the common interests of all the members of the class – but still purely in the economic field. Already at this juncture the problem of the state is posed, but only in terms of winning legal and political equality with the ruling group: 'the right is claimed to participate in legislation and administration, even to reform these – but within the existing fundamental structures.'

3. The third phase is that of hegemony, 'in which one becomes aware that one's own corporate interests, in their present and future development, transcend the corporate limits of the purely economic class, and can and must become the interests of other subordinate groups too'. This is the most purely political phase. It is the phase in which previously germinated ideologies come into conflict until only one of them, or a combination of them, tends to prevail, bringing about a unity of economic, political, intellectual and moral aims, and 'posing all the questions around which the struggle rages not on a corporate but on a "universal" plane, and thus creating the hegemony of a fundamental social group over a series of subordinate groups'.

Gramsci illustrates the first two corporate phases from the experience of a rising capitalist class composed of traders and manufacturers. The development of the working class follows a similar path. The first and most elementary phase is the formation of trade unions to protect the economic interests of different groups and sections. The second phase is when consciousness is reached of the common interests of all members of the working class, when the demand is made for legal and political equality, for legislation to protect trade unions rights and for the right to vote, but within the framework of capitalism.

As the working class moves into the third, hegemonic phase

in which it begins to challenge the hegemony of the capitalist class, more and more workers become aware of the need to take into account the interests of other social groups and classes and to find ways of combining their interests with those of the working class. They begin to develop a political consciousness in place of a corporate consciousness (which Lenin called a 'trade-union consciousness').

In the passage just quoted, Gramsci places the emphasis on the role of ideological struggle – on intellectual and moral reform – in order to achieve a transformation of the outlook of the workers and also of the members of the other classes and groups whose allegiance is needed in order to build up the hegemony of the working class. Hence ideology acts as the 'cement' or cohesive force which binds together a bloc of diverse classes and strata. The nature of ideological struggle – of intellectual and moral reform as Gramsci called it – is further examined in Chapter 8.

Gramsci then passes on to political struggle and the passage already quoted continues:

> It is true that the state is seen as the organ of one particular group, destined to create favourable conditions for the latter's maximum expansion. But the development and expansion of the particular group are conceived of, and presented, as being the motor force of a universal expansion, of a development of all the 'national' energies. In other words, the dominant group is coordinated concretely with the general interests of the subordinate groups, and the life of the state is conceived of as a continuous process of formation and superseding of unstable equilibria (on the juridical plane) between the interests of the fundamental group and those of the subordinate groups – equilibria in which the interests of the dominant group prevail, but only up to a certain point, i.e. stopping short of narrowly corporate economic interest (SPN181-2).

Thus although a hegemonic class predominates in the state, it does not use the state simply as an instrument to impose its interests on those of the other class groups. Rather, the life of the state is seen as a 'continuous process of formation and superseding of unstable equilibria', that is, the state is understood in terms of the complex relations of forces between the two fundamental classes and other classes and social forces. The nature of the state and of power is further considered in Chapter 9.

Summing up the argument so far, it can be said that a class becomes hegemonic in the extent to which it transcends its corporate phase and succeeds in combining the interests of other classes and social forces with its own interests, and in becoming the universal representative of the main social forces which make up the nation.

When a hegemonic class succeeds in constructing a bloc of social forces capable of enduring for an entire historical period, Gramsci calls it a *historic bloc*.

Historical illustrations

One of the questions which Gramsci asks in several passages in the Prison Notebooks is why the medieval communes in Italy – the autonomous city states like Forence, Genoa and Venice – were unable to create a united Italian nation, comparable to the French and English nations under their absolute monarchies. He argued that the answer must be found in understanding why the Italian bourgeoisie of the communes was unable to transcend its economic-corporate phase and create a national state based on its hegemony. This was the problem which was tackled by Machiavelli in his *Modern Prince* (1532); but his plans were never adopted. As Gramsci says: 'An effective Jacobin force was always missing, and could not be constituted; and it was precisely such a Jacobin force which in other nations awakened and organised the national popular collective will' (SPN 131).

What Gramsci means by a Jacobin force is explained in his notes on the French Revolution. He says that the Jacobins strove with determination to ensure a bond between town and country and they succeeded triumphantly. They made the demands of the popular masses their own. They did not concern themselves solely with the immediate and narrow

corporate interests of the bourgeoisie as the hegemonic group
of all the popular forces. They represented not only the needs
and aspirations of the actual physical individuals who
constituted the French bourgoisie, but also the needs of 'all
the national groups which had to be assimilated' to it. This
meant identifying the interests and requirements common to
all the national forces, in order to set these forces in motion
and lead them into the struggle. And at the end of the
eloquent passage in which Gramsci describes the
achievements of the Jacobins (SPN 77-79) he says:

> Not only did they organise a bourgeois government, i.e. make the
> bourgeoisie the dominant class – they did more. They created the
> bourgeois state, made the bourgeoisie into the leading,
> hegemonic class of the nation, in other words gave the new state a
> permanent basis and created the compact modern French nation.

It is arguable that Gramsci's account of the French
Revolution verges on the idealistic. In practice the forging of
the alliance between the Jacobins and the peasantry was
accompanied by many difficulties which led to the use of force
on a considerable scale; conscription had to be used to get the
peasants into the army in sufficient numbers, and a powerful
and highly centralised state apparatus was constructed in the
course of the revolution. But this is fully consistent with
Gramsci's approach, for he holds that the domination of the
bourgeoisie is maintained by a combination of force and
consent – 'hegemony protected by the armour of coercion' – in
a constantly changing balance depending on the actual
conditions at any time.

The balance between coercion and consent was very
different in the Italian Risorgimento, the movement which led
to the unification of Italy in the nineteenth century and to the
ascendancy of the bourgoisie. Gramsci shows that this was
achieved in a very conservative way by the Moderate Party,
which represented the rising bourgeoisie of the Northern
Italian towns, and was at first led by Cavour, prime minister
of the independent state of Piedmont. The principal

instrument for the unification of Italy and the expulsion of the Austrians was the Piedmontese state with its monarchy and army. Thus the process of fundamental social change and creation of a nation was achieved without relying on the democratic struggles of the people and, in particular, without mobilising the peasants against the landowners. Instead, the Moderates forged an alliance with the Southern landowners, leaving the peasants in a state of 'sullen passivity'. The Risorgimento took the form of a revolution from above, which Gramsci called a *passive revolution*. This throws light on the whole process of revolutionary change and is further considered in Chapter 6.

National and international

In considering the relations of forces within any country, international relations have to be taken into account, but as Gramsci insisted, the point of departure must be national:

> In reality, the internal relations of any nation are the result of a combination which is 'original' and (in a certain sense) unique: these relations must be understood and conceived in their originality and uniqueness if one wishes to dominate them and direct them. To be sure, the line of development is towards internationalism, but the point of departure is 'national' – and it is from this point of departure that one must begin (SPN 240).

The recognition that each country must find its own way to socialism in accordance with its own original and unique history and traditions has become widespread since Gramsci's time, and there is no doubt that his own political activities and writings have made a major contribution towards this understanding. The great impact of the factory councils' movement was possible because it was not a mechanical application of the Russian soviets to Italy, but a creative adaptation of the experiences of the Russian Revolution to the very different Italian conditions. (It is examined in Chapter 10.) The defeat of the factory councils movement in 1920 led

Gramsci to make a deeper study of the special features of the Italian liberal state which had disintegrated under the impact of fascism; and this study took shape in the 'Lyons theses' which were presented by Gramsci and Togliatti to the Third Congress of the Italian Communist Party in 1926 and also in Gramsci's unfinished essay on the Southern Question (SPW II 343-349 and 441-63). This analysis of Italian conditions became one of his main preoccupations in prison, reflected in his notes on Italian history, Italian literature and the Italian language, and in the immense number of notes on Italian intellectuals which are scattered throughout the Prison Notebooks. The path to socialism could only be found on the basis of a thorough understanding of the 'original and unique' history of Italy.

The impact of the Russian Revolution of 1917 was so great that it was natural for revolutionaries in other countries in the years immediately following to think that the socialist revolution in their countries would have the same essential features as it had had in Russia – features which eventually came to be embodied in the term 'dictatorship of the proletariat'. What is much more remarkable is that some people still take the same view more than sixty years after the Russian Revolution. In this connection it is important to remember the amount of time that Lenin devoted to studying the special characteristics of Russian capitalism as it developed out of feudalism in the closing years of the last century. This study absorbed a large part of his energies during the first years of his political life and culminated in the publication in 1899 of his book *The Development of Capitalism in Russia*. Neil Harding, in his penetrating study of Lenin, has said that this book is 'arguably the most important' that Lenin ever wrote[8]. The theoretical conclusions he drew from it were the foundation for his political strategy in the years that followed.

Lenin once said that 'the most essential thing in Marxism is the concrete analysis of concrete conditions' and that genuine dialectics consists in 'a thorough detailed analaysis of a process'. In stressing the necessity for studying the original and unique history of one's own country, Gramsci was only following in the footsteps of Lenin. His concept of hegemony was a new tool, developed out of his own experiences and his study of Italian, French and Russian history, for analysing the complex relations of forces existing at any time. 'It is necessary,' he also wrote, 'to draw attention violently to the present as it is, if one wants to transform it' (Q 1131). A revolutionary party should continually make a cool, scientific analysis of the strength of the opposing forces as well as of its own, verging on pessimism. This should form the basis for working out and taking political initiatives, verging on optimism, in the spirit of Gramsci's favourite motto: pessimism of the intelligence, optimism of the will.[9]

4   The Maintenance of Hegemony

Organic crises

In the previous chapter hegemony was described mainly in terms of the rise to power of a revolutionary class, and the three historical examples which were mentioned – two from Italy and one from France – concerned the achievement of hegemony by the capitalist class. Of equal importance is the maintenance of hegemony *after* state power has been gained. As Gramsci says in the passage already quoted (p. 22), even when a social group has become dominant and holds power firmly in its grasp, it must continue to 'lead' as well. Hegemony can never be taken for granted, but has to be continually fought for afresh. This requires persistent activities to maintain and strengthen the social authority of the ruling class in all areas of civil society, and the making of such compromises as are needed to adapt the existing system of alliances to changing conditions and to the activities of the opposing forces.

This process can be seen at work most clearly in periods when the hegemony of the ruling political forces is endangered and is tending to disintegrate. There may ensue a fairly prolonged period of instability and transition, during which the system of alliances forming the basis for the hegemony of the ruling groups may have to undergo far-reaching changes and a process of restructuring if it is to survive. Gramsci insists on the importance of distinguishing between *organic* changes which are relatively permanent, and those which appear as occasional, immediate and almost accidental:

A crisis occurs, sometimes lasting for decades. This exceptional duration means that incurable structural contradictions have

revealed themselves (reached maturity) and that, despite this, the
political forces which are struggling to conserve and defend the
existing structure itself are making every effort to cure them,
within certain limits, and to overcome them. These incessant and
persistent efforts ... form the terrain of the 'conjunctural' and it is
upon this terrain that the forces of opposition organise (SPN
178).

The term *conjuncture* is more widely used on the continent than
in Britain; it is what Lenin used to call 'the current situation'
or the balance of political forces existing at the present
moment to which political tactics have to be applied. What
Gramsci wishes to stress is that the current situation is to be
understood, not only in terms of the immediate economic and
political problems, but also in the 'incessant and persistent
efforts' which are made to conserve and defend the existing
system. If the crisis is deep – an organic one – these efforts
cannot be purely defensive. They will consist in the struggle to
create a new balance of political forces, requiring a reshaping
of state institutions as well as the formation of new ideologies;
and if the forces of opposition are not strong enough to shift
the balance of forces decisively in their direction, the
conservative forces will succeed in building a new system of
alliances which will reestablish their hegemony. Beneath the
surface of the day-to-day events, an organic and relatively
permanent, structural change will have taken place.

One conclusion that Gramsci draws from these
considerations is that 'a social form always has marginal
possibilities for further development and organisational
improvement, and in particular can count on the relative
weakness of the rival progressive force as a result of its specific
character and way of life. It is necessary for the dominant social
force to preserve this weakness' (SPN 222).

The organic crisis with which Gramsci was centrally
concerned was the crisis in Italy, lasting from about 1910 to
1921, which was eventually resolved by the rise of Mussolini's
fascism. In his notes on Italian history Gramsci analyses the
shifting system of compromises which had enabled the

Northern industrialists, in alliance with the Southern landowners, to maintain a limited hegemony in the framework of the Italian liberal state from the time of the Risorgimento (SPN 52-120).[10] Between 1910 and 1912, however, there began a profound unheaval in the structure of Italian society affecting all classes and the whole of Italian culture; it was marked by a big rise in the militancy of the working class and of sections of the peasantry, by a growth of nationalism and the imperialist adventure in Libya, as well as by important shifts in the Catholic movement. Under the impact of the First World War and its aftermath, the system of alliances which had ensured the hegemony of the Northern industrialists disintegrated. The much greater strength of the working-class movement, with its revolutionary tendencies, contributed to this disintegration, but the movement was still mainly under reformist leadership, and was unable to build an alliance with the different social forces capable of presenting an effective challenge to the ruling groups. There was a 'crisis of authority' – a crisis of hegemony – consisting in the fact 'that the old is dying and the new cannot be born'.

In these conditions fascism found a mass basis in the urban and rural petty bourgeoisie who had become much more politically active as a result of the war, and could easily be organised into military-style squads for brutal attacks on the labour movement and its institutions. Mussolini's fascist movement thus succeeded in replacing the old compromises by reorganising all the bourgeoisie's forces in a single political organism combining the party, the government and the state, cemented by a reactionary ideology based on aggressive nationalism. The working-class movement was defeated, not only by a resort to violent repression and by the passivity of the reformist leadership, but also by the ability of the capitalist class to reorganise its forces in a new way, in spite of a serious economic crisis.

In the past 150 years of British history it is possible to distinguish three main periods of transition which may qualify as organic crises in Gramscian terms, and which will be considered in Chapter 7.

The theme of this chapter has been that once a class or social group has achieved hegemony, the system of alliances on which that hegemony is based (historic bloc) has to be continually readjusted and re-negotiated. Periodically there may develop an organic crisis in which the historic bloc begins to disintegrate, creating the opportunity for a subordinate class to transcend its corporate limitations and build up a broad movement capable of challenging the existing order and achieving hegemony; but if the opportunity is not taken, the balance of forces will shift back to the dominant class which will re-establish its hegemony on the basis of a new pattern of alliances.

Caesarism

A crisis of hegemony may have profound effects on political parties and on the form of the state. As Gramsci says, 'social classes become detached from their traditional parties' and organisational forms and the people who lead them 'are no longer recognised by their class (or fraction of a class) as its expression'. There is a crisis of representation. When such crises occur, 'the immediate situation becomes delicate and dangerous, because the field is open for violent solutions, for the activities of unknown forces, represented by charismatic "men of destiny"' (SPN p. 210). Gramsci used the term 'Caesarism' to denote the outcome of 'a situation in which the forces in conflict balance each other in a catastrophic manner, that is to say, in such a way that a continuation of the conflict can only result in their reciprocal destruction.' (SPN. 219).

Gramsci suggested that Caesarism does not always have the same historical significance. It can take both progressive and reactionary forms. Caesar and Napoleon I are examples of progressive Caesarism. Napoleon III and Bismarck of reactionary Caesarism. Besides the fascist regimes of Mussolini and Hitler, there have been a great variety of exceptional forms of state, such as the colonels' regime in Greece, which qualify as forms of Caesarism.

Gramsci also pointed out that a Caesarist solution can arise even without a Caesar, without any great, 'heroic' and representative personality. 'The parliamentary system has also provided a mechanism for such compromise solutions (SPN 220). In other words, a Caesarist outcome may not be 'catastrophic' involving the immediate violent repression of one side by the other, the destruction of democratic rights and the creation of an exceptional form of state. Instead, there may be a shift towards a more authoritarian form of parliamentary government through a succession of stages (which might ultimately lead to an exceptional form of state). In Britain since the 1970s there has been developing a situation of stalemate between the opposing classes in which 'the old is dying and the new cannot be born'. A shift to the right within the Conservative Party was reflected in the election in 1976 of Margaret Thatcher as leader. There were significant authoritarian elements in the ideology of 'Thatcherism' and in the measures taken by the Thatcher government, such as the legislative attacks on the trade unions and local authorities, and the strengthening of the police and the armed forces. It does not seem justifiable at this stage to characterise this approach as a Caesarist one, but the possibility of a Caesarist outcome of Britain's present organic crisis cannot be excluded. The changes in the relations of forces, and in the system of representation, which were developing in the late 1970s and early 1980s are considered further in Chapter 7.

5   National-popular

In previous chapters it was argued that if a class is to become hegemonic, it has to transcend its economic-corporate phase by taking into account the aims and interests of other classes and social forces, linking these with its own interests so as to become their universal representative. However, the nature of these 'social forces' has not yet been discussed. We can now take a crucial further step. A class cannot achieve national leadership, and become a hegemonic class, *if it confines itself only to class interests*; it must also take into account the popular and democratic aspirations and struggles of the people which do not have a necessary class character.

In Gramsci's important note on the relation of forces quoted in Chapter 3, he says that the development and expansion of a class aspiring to hegemony is 'conceived of and presented as being the motor force of a universal expansion, of a development of all the national energies' (SPN p.182). And in describing the decisive role played by the Jacobins in the creation of the French nation, he stresses the popular nature of the hegemony they established 'which in other nations awakened and organised the national-popular collective will, and founded modern states' (SPN 131). Thus hegemony has a *national-popular* dimension as well as a class dimension. As Gramsci says 'It is in the concept of hegemony that those exigencies which are national in character are knotted together' (SPN 241).

For example, a nation which is oppressed by another develops traditions of struggle for national liberation, and indeed in the course of history the pepeo of every country develop powerful ideas, expressed by terms like 'patriotism' and 'nationalism' which can, as Gramsci says, have the force of popular religions. A hegemonic class is one which succeeds in combining these patriotic struggles and ideas with its own class interests so as to achieve national leadership. Many historical illustrations spring to mind, in addition to the Jacobins in the French Revolution: to take only one, the Chinese workers and peasants under the leadership of the Chinese Communist Party combined the national struggle against the Japanese with social revolution.

The great variety of movements for democratic rights, for freedom of speech and the right to vote and for many other kinds of civil liberties, which the British people have engaged in over many centuries, cannot be *reduced* to class struggles even though they have been closely related to them. Many of these struggles reflect a conflict between the people and the government, or 'officialdom', which is not the same as the conflict between working class and capitalist class arising directly from the relations of production. The relation between democratic struggles and class struggles is a vast subject which is opened up by the Gramscian concept of popular-national.[11] It has been suggested, for example, that the strength of Chartism in the 1830s and 1840s was due to the link which it established between the inherited tradition of radical politics and a developing practice of class struggle[12].

After the period of Chartism, however, the British bourgeoisie was particularly successful in achieving leadership in the process of broadening parliamentary democracy and in strengthening its hegemony by this means. This led many communists and others in the past, and Lenin's influence was especially strong here, to take the view that parliamentary democracy was an instrument of the capitalist class, and to counterpose to it direct democracy in the form of soviets, shop stewards' committees and the like; and this is still the view taken on the whole by ultra-leftists. A socialist revolution, according to this view, requires the replacement of parliamentary democracy by direct democracy, rather than a combination of both. In consequence a whole sphere of democratic struggle is surrendered to the other side. Instead, parliament and everything associated with it should be seen as a vital terrain, on which the struggle for political and ideological hegemony takes place. The fact is that the authority of the House of Commons has been gravely undermined by a series of developments in the present century – the shift of power to the cabinet, to the prime minister within the cabinet, and to the upper layer of civil servants, for example – and is in danger of being still further eroded as a result of the authoritarian tendencies which have gained ground in the Conservative Party. There are, therefore, particularly good opportunities now opening up for the labour movement to take the lead in strengthening parliamentary democracy, as well as direct democracy.

There are many other social movements, apart from the struggle for civil liberties, which have their own specific qualities and do not have a necessary class character. The movements which express the demands of women, students, young people, ethnic minorities; the anti-nuclear weapons movement; the various ecological movements concerned with the environment; community activities of many kinds concerned with aspects of health, education, housing and other issues. What all these movements have in common is that they do not arise directly out of the relations of production. Their position has been well described by Laclau and Mouffe:

> Their enemy is defined not by its function of exploitation, but by wielding a certain power. And this power, too, does not derive from a place in the relations of production, but is the outcome of a form of organisation characteristic of the present society. This society is indeed capitalist, but this is not its only characteristic; it is sexist and patriarchal as well, not to mention racist.[13]

There are therefore a variety of popular democratic struggles which have their own specific qualities and cannot be reduced to the class struggle although they are related to it in various ways; and the struggle to gain the leadership of these popular-democratic, non-class aspirations of the people is an essential part of the contest for hegemony between the working class and the capitalist class. These aspirations, and the movements which express them, constitute a political terrain which is fought over by the two fundamental classes contending for hegemony. If the working class is to achieve hegemony, it needs patiently to build up a network of alliances with these social movements; and the process of building these alliances is an essential part of what Gramsci called the *war of position*. These alliances must respect the autonomy of the movements, so that each of them is able to make its own special contribution towards the new socialist society. The concept of war of position is more fully examined in Chapter 13 on revolutionary strategy.

The distinction between class struggles and conflicts which do not have a necessary class character is not explicitly made in the Prison Notebooks though it is implicit in Gramsci's conception of national-popular. It was first made, as far as I am aware, by Ernesto Laclau in his essay 'Fascism and Ideology' and is perhaps the most valuable advance in elaborating the concept of hegemony which has been made since the publication of the Prison Notebooks.[14]

To sum up, the process of transcending the corporate phase and advancing towards hegemony has two main aspects. First, the working class can only become hegemonic if it gains the leadership of an alliance of classes and strata – the aspect which is derived from Leninism. Second, it must unite popular-democratic struggles with its own struggle against the capitalist class so as to build up a national-popular collective will; this is one of the major contributions which Gramsci made to the concept of hegemony.[15]

This initial exposition of the meaning of national-popular has been made in terms of the unification of struggles and movements, but the process is in reality inseparable from changes in the outlook and consciousness of those who are involved or, as Gramsci put it, from intellectual and moral reform. This is explored in Chapter 8 on ideology.

6   Passive Revolution

The Risorgimento

Gramsci's analysis of the contrast between the French Revolution and the Italian Risorgimento (referred to on p. 33) led him to develop the concept of *passive revolution*. In the French Revolution the Jacobins were able to mobilise the people for the revolutionary struggle through supporting the demands of the peasantry and building an alliance with them. In contrast, the unification of Italy and the rise to power of the Italian bourgeoisie in the Risorgimento was carried out by Cavour and the Moderate Party in a very different way, with the minimum reliance on popular struggles; their main instrument was the Piedmontese state with its army, its monarchy and its bureaucracy.

The liberal-democratic current was represented by the Action Party of Mazzini and Garibaldi, but it played a subordinate role to the Moderates; and the principal reason for this, in Gramsci's view, was that it failed to develop a programme reflecting the essential demands of the popular masses, and in the first place of the peasantry. Thus the Action Party never succeeded in stamping the Risorgimento with a popular and democratic character. Instead the Moderates, with the aid of their own intellectuals, exercised a powerful attractive force over intellectuals throughout the peninsula, and succeeded in using the national question to unite all the different sections of the Italian bourgeoisie under their leadership. The Moderates reinforced their ascendancy over the Action Party by the method which became known in Italy as *transformism*, and involved the 'gradual but continuous absorption, achieved by methods which varied in their effectiveness, of the active elements produced by allied groups – and even of those which came from antagonistic groups' (SPN 58-9). For example, Gramsci says that in the period from 1860 to 1900 individual figures formed by the democratic opposition parties were incorporated individually into the conservative-moderate political class, characterised by its aversion to any intervention of the popular masses in state life; from 1900 onwards entire groups from the democratic opposition passed over into the moderate camp.

Thus the Moderates established their hegemony over the Action Party and over the whole movement of the Risorgimento, but the process of national unification and the rise to power of the northern capitalists was achieved without relying on popular struggles. No attempt was made to coordinate the interests of the peasants and of other subordinate classes with those of the bourgeoisie so as to create a national-popular collective will. The majority of the peasants remained under the influence of the Roman Catholic church which was hostile to the new Italian state (having lost the Papal Territories). The Risorgimento took the form of a 'revolution from above', carried out mainly through the agency of the Piedmontese state. The strategy adopted by the Italian bourgeoisie had the character of a *passive revolution*. The Moderates only established their hegemony over the Action Party; in other words, there was hegemony of part of the capitalist class over the whole of that class, combined with an absence of hegemony over the peasants and the great majority of the population. As Gramsci put it, there was 'dictatorship without hegemony'.

One aspect of a passive revolution deserves special emphasis. Referring to the role of the Piedmont state, Gramsci says 'The important thing is to analyse more profoundly the significance of a 'Piedmont'-type function in passive revolutions – i.e. the fact that a state replaces the local social groups in leading a struggle for renewal' (SPN 105). In a passive revolution the state is substituted for the political (hegemonic) activity of the class; the greater the degree of passive revolution in any situation, the more does this process of *substitution* takes place.

In setting out Gramsci's analysis of the Risorgimento, an extremely simplified picture of a very complex historical period has been given, very much more simplified than that given by Gramsci in his Prison Notebooks. The people were not entirely passive in the Risorgimento which included many heroic episodes, such as the risings in Milan and Rome in 1848-49 and Garibaldi's expedition to Sicily in 1860. But in its overall character the Risorgimento was a passive revolution which did not have a national-popular quality. Gramsci sums up the result (SPN 90): the leaders of the Risorgimento 'were aiming at the creation of a modern state in Italy and in fact produced a bastard'. They did not succeed either in stimulating the formation of an extensive and energetic ruling class or in integrating the people into the framework of the new state. The Italian bourgeoisie could only achieve a limited measure of hegemony, and the subsequent history of Italy was marked by a system of compromises which were unstable and lacking in popular support. Gramsci considered that the weakness of the Italian liberal state founded by the Risorgimento was one of the factors which made possible the rise of fascism in the 1920s.

The concept of passive revolution

Having developed the notion of passive revolution out of his analysis of the Risorgimento and the subsequent history of the Italian state, Gramsci takes a further step. He suggests that passive revolution is not only an interpretation of the Risorgimento but also of 'every epoch characterised by complex upheavals'. Whenever the hegemony of the bourgeoisie begins to disintegrate and a period of organic crisis develops, the process of reorganisation which is needed to re-establish its hegemony will to some extent have the character of a passive revolution. In his series of notes collected under the heading 'Americanism and Fordism' he detected an element of passive revolution in Roosevelt's New

Deal, consisting of the great expansion in state intervention to help overcome the profound economic crisis of the 1930s. There was also a considerable growth of state intervention in Italy under Mussolini's fascist regime:

> There is a passive revolution involved in the fact that – through legislative intervention of the state, and by means of corporative organisation – relatively far-reaching modifications are being introduced into the country's economic structure ... [In Italy] this could be the only solution whereby to develop the productive forces under the direction of the traditional ruling classes in competition with the more advanced industrial formations of countries ... It thus reinforces the hegemonic system and the forces of military and civil coercion at the disposal of the traditional ruling classes (SPN 119-20).

Thus fascism in Italy was a form of passive revolution whereby necessary reforms in the economic structure were carried out from above, through the agency of the state.

Gramsci suggests therefore, that passive revolution is the characteristic response to an organic crisis. Passive revolution is involved whenever relatively far-reaching modifications in a country's economic structure are made from above, through the agency of the state apparatuses, without relying on the active participation of the people[16].

The concept of passive revolution can be extended to cover the analysis of socialist as well as bourgeois revolutions. In the transition to socialism, the strategy of the working class must have the character of an *anti-passive revolution*, based on an extension of class struggles and of popular-democratic struggles so as to mobilise ever-wider sections of the population for democratic reforms. The development of this anti-passive strategy requires a deeper analysis of civil society – the sphere of class and popular-democratic struggles. The relation between civil society and the state in the transition to socialism is explored in Chapter 9.

In the next chapter, Gramsci's concepts of hegemony and of organic crisis are discussed in the light of British history.

7   Three Organic Crises in Britain

The 1830s and 1840s

In Chapter 4 the discussion of Gramsci's concept of organic crisis was illustrated by the crisis in Italian society lasting from about 1910 to 1921, when it was resolved by the rise of fascism. Coming nearer home, it is possible to distinguish at least three periods of transition in the past 150 years of British history which may qualify as organic crises in Gramscian terms. The following remarks are necessarily tentative and sketchy, and greatly oversimplify a complex historical process, but may serve to illustrate the ways in which the British ruling class has maintained its hegemony when confronted with profound economic and social changes and with the growing strength of the working class movement.

The first of these crises of hegemony was in the second quarter of the nineteenth century when the rapid growth of factory industry and of the urban population, combined with all the other changes brought about by the industrial revolution, gave rise to a serious disequilibrium in the political structures inherited from the previous century. For the first time in British history a powerful working-class movement emerged, compounded of the radical democratic tradition of Paine and Cobbett, Luddism, and early trade unionism, and above all the new social force of Chartism. The old ways of ruling were becoming unworkable, and the 1830s and 1840s witnessed a prolonged struggle to elaborate new methods. Part of the answer was the creation of more effective coercive institutions such as the new police forces and the new Poor

Law. But what was notable about the mid-Victorian period was the degree to which the urban bourgeoisie was able to gain consent to its leadership in society through a willingness to make the necessary compromises and concessions. It was certainly helped by the division within the working class caused by the emergence of an upper stratum of skilled workers and the reformist outlook they developed. But the key to its success was that the skilled workers achieved a measure of representation within society through the development of their own organisations, especially trade unions, co-operative and friendly societies. The relative stability of the new system rested on the recognition of the autonomy of these new working-class institutions, so that consent to the leadership of the ruling class was actively and spontaneously generated rather than imposed from above. The growth of this autonomous working-class movement under reformist leaders (who were ready to engage in hard-fought trade-union struggles but did not challenge the basic assumptions of capitalism) prepared the way for the extension of the vote in 1867 and 1884. As Robert Gray has written: 'Britain is in many ways the "classic" country, both of democratic struggle (from the English Revolution to the Chartists and beyond) and of its incorporation into political life under bourgeois leadership.'[17]

There were of course many other factors (such as the development of modern political parties in the shape of the Liberal and Conservative Parties, alternating in office), which contributed to the hegemony of the British ruling class after Chartism died down. But the question of autonomy for working-class organisations deserves special emphasis. A ruling class is more authentically hegemonic the more it leaves the subordinate classes scope for organising themselves into autonomous social forces. The labour movement in a country such as Britain will only be able to mount an effective challenge to the hegemony of the capitalist class if it builds up a broad alliance of social forces under its leadership, based on a genuine recognition that the autonomy of these social forces must be respected, and that they each have their own

contribution to make to the new socialist strategy. This is a
crucial aspect of revolutionary strategy – Gramsci's war of
position – which will be taken up again in later chapters.

From about 1910 to 1945

In the years from about 1910 to 1914 the stability of British
political life was severely shaken by a series of massive popular
movements. The struggle between capital and labour reached
a new pitch of intensity in a number of great national strikes
by miners, railwaymen, dockers and others. There was also the
militant campaign of the suffragettes led by the Pankhursts for
the extension of the vote to women; and the rise of the Irish
national movement leading to the Home Rule Bill, bitterly
opposed by the Protestant minority in Ulster, and culminating
in the Curragh Mutiny of British army officers in Ireland
which was openly supported by Tory party leaders in
England. There was a crisis of political authority and of the
nineteenth century constitutionalism based on the alternation
in office of the Conservative and Liberal parties – a new
organic crisis in Gramsci's terms. During the years following
the outbreak of war in 1914 the old system was slowly
reconstructed to emerge as a new political settlement. The
replacement of the Liberal Party as the main opposition party
by the Labour Party under social-democratic leadership,
committed to parliament, was the most obvious change. But
two other features were very significant. First, a new system
for the representation of labour developed outside parliament;
trade union leaders were drawn into the state machinery in
various ways, appointed to boards and tribunals, consulted
and negotiated with by ministers and civil servants.
Employers' organisations were treated in the same way, and
this resulted in the gradual evolution of the system which has
become known as 'tripartism', or as 'corporatism' because it
provides for the corporate representation of capital and
labour. (The term 'corporate' is here used in a different sense
from Gramsci's term 'economic-corporate' which refers to a
stage in the development of a class.) The second new feature

was the extension of the social and economic activities of the state, which had already received its first big impulse under the Liberal governments of 1906-14.

These two major developments – tripartism and the expansion of the state – were compromises which did not at that time threaten the foundations of capitalism but which contributed to a new equilibrium of social forces, a new form of 'permanently organised consent'. This was established on a much firmer basis during the Second World War and by the Labour Governments of 1945-51, with the setting up of the National Health Service and of a much-improved system of social security, with the vital addition of a commitment to full employment. When the Conservative Party re-established its dominant position in the 1950s it did so on the basis of an acceptance of corporatism, the 'welfare state' and full employment. In the 1950s and 1960s British workers made substantial gains in the shape of higher living standards and better social services, while the trade-union movement was growing stronger, especially through the extension of workplace organisation in conditions of full employment. Nevertheless, the working class remained in the economic-corporate stage, and did not mount a serious challenge to the hegemony of the British capitalist class.

An essential condition for the success of this 'corporate' representation of the working class was the dominant influence of social democracy in the leadership of the trade unions and the Labour Party. Central to the ideology and practice of social democracy is its belief that the state is the neutral arbiter between classes; through winning a parliamentary majority, concessions can be obtained in the shape of social reforms which promote the ideals of 'social justice' and 'equality'. Social democracy is therefore opposed to the mobilisation of the people to exert pressure through extra-parliamentary methods of struggle. There is no need for such methods, for reforms can be carried out through the agency of the state. Holding these beliefs, the right-wing leaders of the Labour Party and the trade unions were able to win the workers for economic policies which strengthen capitalism, gaining their consent to these policies through the offer of social reforms. This is the social-democratic form of what Gramsci called a *passive revolution* – the making of relatively far-reaching modifications in a country's economic and social structure from above, through the manipulation and expansion of the state, without relying on the active participation of the people. The characteristics of British social democracy are further discussed in Chapter 13.

The 1970s onwards

The system of corporatism, accompanied by full employment and the expansion of the 'welfare state' worked well enough during the 1950s when British industry was able to benefit from the growth of world trade before the war-ravaged economies of continental Europe and Japan had recovered. But in the 1960s British manufacturing industry, deprived of its former protection in the privileged markets of the Empire, was exposed to the full blast of competition from rival capitalist powers and its relative weakness was more and more revealed. During the years of the Labour governments under Harold Wilson from 1964 to 1970, the making of concessions on which corporatism depended became more difficult and there were signs of growing tension between the government and the trade unions. Meanwhile, a New Right was beginning to take shape within the Conservative Party, which rejected corporatism and the search for consensus with the trade union movement, and favoured instead a greater reliance on market forces, major reductions in welfare services and in state intervention in the economy, and legislation to weaken the trade unions who were seen as the principal obstruction to the free play of market forces.

The Conservative government of 1970-74 under Edward Heath reflected this new approach when it launched an attack on the trade unions with the Industrial Relations Act 1971; but it failed to overcome the determined resistance of the trade union movement, demonstrating the remarkable defensive strength it had acquired after three decades of full employment and the rise of the shop-stewards' movement. There followed a new phase of corporatism under the 1974-79 governments of Wilson and Callaghan; incomes policies were pursued in the novel form of the social contract, under which the TUC was offered consultation on a wide range of policies by the government, while in return it was expected to secure the compliance of its members with incomes policies involving wage restraint. In face of the worsening economic crisis, the Callaghan government adopted a strategy of severe deflation and public expenditure cuts, accompanied by a big rise in unemployment. The system of corporatism was much discredited, for it depended on social reform and better living standards which it had failed to deliver. The performance of the British economy compared with its main capitalist rivals continued to deteriorate.

During the Callaghan years the shift to the right in the Conservative Party, following the election of Margaret Thatcher as its leader in 1976, was greatly strengthened. The New Right of the 1960s developed into the more effective 'Thatcherism', consisting of three main strands. First, it rejected the Keynesian methods of running the economy with the aim of securing full employment that were followed by Labour and Conservative governments alike during the long post-war boom. Instead, it adopted an extreme form of monetarist doctrine: the government was not responsible for what happened to the economy but only for maintaining sound money, free competition and the security of property and contract; the source of economic prosperity was individual enterprise, and government activities should be reduced to a minimum. Second, since trade unions obstructed the free working of market forces, their legal rights had to be severely curtailed in order to shift the balance of bargaining power in favour of the employers; the system of corporatism was to be ended. The democratic elements in the state were to be further weakened by a strengthening of the police and the armed forces.

The third strand of Thatcherism was a new emphasis on ideology, exploiting the popular feelings of resentment with

many of the aspects of the 'welfare state': the arbitrary
decisions of state bureaucracies and nationalised industries,
the burden of taxation, 'welfare scroungers', the 'privileges'
enjoyed by immigrants, and the disorder created by strikes
and demonstrations. Thatcherism skilfully worked on
traditional conservative elements of popular morality
concerning the family, authority, standards, and self-reliance,
elements which formed part of what Gramsci called common
sense – the confused and often contradictory way in which a
person perceives the world. The central theme was the posing
of all questions of government policy as problems of individual
responsibility and individual choice, to be exercised within a
framework of 'law and order'.[18] This attempt to integrate
traditional conservative elements of popular morality into an
ideology centred on individual self-help and private enterprise
is a good illustration of the process of ideological struggle
considered in the next chapter.

The oversimplified populist slogans of Thatcherism proved
effective in shifting the balance of forces in the country to the
right and in helping the Conservative Party to win a decisive
victory in the election of 1979; but the task of putting the
slogans into effect was more difficult. The extreme form of
monetarism adopted by the Thatcher government proved
disastrous for the British economy with registered
unemployment rising beyond three million in the winter of
1981-82. The move to the right within the Conservative Party,
together with the growing strength of the left in the Labour
Party under the leadership of Tony Benn, created conditions
in which the new Social Democratic Party came into
existence, aiming to reconstruct the social-democratic centre
in a new way, in alliance with the Liberal Party rather than
the trade union movement.

Thus by the end of the 1970s British capitalism entered a
period, not only of economic crisis, but also of organic crisis in
Gramsci's sense of the term. The system of political
representation, which had served to ensure the hegemony of
the capitalist class for the previous fifty years, began to
disintegrate, and an intensive search for a new system, a new

alignment of political and social forces, was pursued. This creates great opportunities for the advance to socialism, but unless they can be seized by the labour movement so as to build up a system of alliances under its leadership, acting as a magnet for new social forces and creating a national-popular collective will, the political representatives of capital may succeed in re-establishing their hegemony in a new way.

8 Ideology

The materiality of ideology

The term ideology has often been used to mean simply a system of ideas, as for instance when people refer to liberal or conservative or socialist ideology. For Gramsci, ideology is more than a system of ideas. He distinguishes between the arbitrary systems worked out by particular intellectuals or philosophers, and historically organic ideologies, that is, those which are necessary to a given social formation: 'To the extent that ideologies are historically necessary they have a validity which is psychological; they "organise" human masses, and create the terrain on which men move, acquire consciousness of their position, struggle, etc.' (SPN 367) Ideologies are not individual fancies, but are embodied in collective and communal modes of living. And Gramsci refers to the affirmation made by Marx about the 'solidity of popular beliefs'.

Ideology is therefore not something which, as it were, floats in the air high above the political and other practical activities of men and women. On the contrary, it has a material existence in these practical activities. It provides people with rules of practical conduct and moral behaviour, and is equivalent to 'a religion understood in the secular sense of a unity of faith between a conception of the world and a corresponding norm of conduct' (SPN 326).

Gramsci points out that there is often a contradiction between the philosophy, or conception of the world, or religion which a person consciously believes, and one's mode of conduct, and he asks 'which therefore is one's real conception of the world – that which is logically affirmed as an intellectual choice, or that which emerges from the real activity of each person and which is implicit in his or her mode of action?' (SPN 326) The necessary transformation of political consciousness required for the advance to socialism has to be moral as well as intellectual and that is why Gramsci calls for a 'moral and intellectual' reform as an essential element of the hegemony of the working class.

In reading the Prison Notebooks it is helpful to bear in mind that Gramsci uses a variety of terms which for him are broadly equivalent to ideology, such as culture, philosophy, world outlook, or conception of the world, as well as the phrase 'moral and intellectual reform' when he is dealing with the transformation of ideology required for the advance to socialism.

There is another important aspect of the material nature of ideology. Ideological practice possesses its own agents in the shape of intellectuals who specialise in the elaboration of organic ideologies and in the task of moral and intellectual reform. In his note on the Risorgimento Gramsci shows how the leaders of the Moderate Party successfully carried out this task for the Italian bourgeoisie through building an ideological bloc which exercised a powerful attraction throughout the country. They acted as the 'organic intellectuals' of the Italian bourgeoisie because they performed this vital function for it. So he argues that every fundamental class 'creates one or more strata of intellectuals who give it homogeneity and an awareness of its own function not only in the economic but also in the political and social fields' (SPN 5). Thus the working class must also create its own organic intellectuals if it is to succeed in becoming hegemonic. The vital role of intellectuals and of a revolutionary party as a 'collective intellectual' is further discussed in Chapters 12 and 14.

To sum up the argument so far, ideologies have a material existence in the sense that they are embodied in the social practices of individuals and in the institutions and organisations within which these social practices take place. These organisations include the political parties, trade unions and other organisations forming part of civil society; the various apparatuses of the state; and economic organisations such as industrial and commercial companies and financial institutions. All these bodies play a part in elaborating, sustaining and spreading ideologies; or in other words, they have ideological effects. It is important to recognise that this applies to state apparatuses as well as to the organisations of civil society; for example, the ideological effects of the law and the legal system are very influential; the law does not only have a coercive effect. Lastly, it must be stressed that ideologies are not to be reduced to social practices; they not only have a material existence, but they also exist in and through ideas, through the relations of concepts and propositions.

Ideology as cement

Gramsci considers that an ideology is not to be judged by its truth or falsity but by its efficacy in binding together a bloc of diverse social elements, and in acting as cement or as an agent of social unification. A hegemonic class is one which succeeds in combining the interests of other classes, groups and movements with its own interests so as to create a national-popular collective will. In the previous chapter this was discussed in terms of the political leadership required to overcome all the narrow, corporate prejudices of a fundamental class and to make all necessary compromises in political and economic programmes in order to build up and sustain a bloc of social forces, aspiring towards a new historic bloc. There is also a crucial ideological dimension in the building of such a bloc. A collective will can only be forged by a process of intellectual and moral reform that will create a common conception of the world. There must be 'a cultural-social unity through which a multiplicity of dispersed wills, with heterogeneous aims, are welded together with a single aim, as the basis of an equal and common conception of the world' (SPN 349).

However, this new common conception of the world will not

be a purely capitalist or a purely monopoly capitalist one in the case of the bourgeoisie; nor will it be a socialist ideology representing in a pure form the outlook of the working class. The illusion that characterises the ultra-left is that the working class will eventually come to adopt Marxism in a pure form as its ideology. Instead, there has to be a more complex synthesis of class objectives with themes that have arisen out of the original and unique history of each country. As we saw in the previous chapter, if a class is to become hegemonic it has to succeed in combining these popular-democratic themes, which are rooted in the history of each country and which do not have a necessary class character, with its own class objectives in order to create a national-popular will. For this is the only way in which the ideas and aims of a revolutionary class can become deeply rooted among the people.

How is this to be done? It is not a matter of starting from scratch to build up a new ideological system out of entirely new elements. Gramsci sees it rather as a process of criticism of the existing ideological complex:

> This criticism makes possible a process of differentiation and change in the relative weight that the elements of the old ideologies used to possess. What was previously secondary and subordinate, or even incidental, is now taken to be primary – becomes the nucleus of a new ideological and theoretical complex. The old collective will dissolves into its contradictory elements since the subordinate ones develop socially, etc. (SPN 195).

Thus the nature of ideological struggle is not to make a completely fresh start. Rather, it is a process of transformation in which some of the elements are rearranged and combined in a different way with a new nucleus or central principle. A process of this kind is necessary because, if the old ideological system was a genuinely popular one, then the elements (or at least some of them) to which this popularity was due, need to be preserved in the new system even if their relative weight and some of their content is changed. The unity of the new ideological system will stem from its nucleus or central unifying principle.[19]

The task of intellectual and moral reform facing the working class is, therefore, to combine these diverse ideological elements, some of which may not have a class character, with the socialist values which express the fundamental interests of the working class. This ideological struggle is the counterpart of the political struggle to build a national-popular collective will which was discussed in Chapter 5.

One illustration of this process would be the way in which the popular feelings of national identity and patriotism are combined into an ideological system. This can be done in a great variety of ways: in an aggressive, nationalist style, as it was in German and Italian fascism; in a way which assumes a natural superiority over other nations and a right of international leadership, as it was by the British ruling class in the last century; or in a movement for national liberation linked with fundamental themes of social advance as was successfully done by the Chinese Communist Party in the struggle against Japanese imperialism; and so on.

Another illustration from Britain is the way in which the shift to the right in the Conservative Party around a new type of 'authoritarian populism' (referred to in Chapter 6, p. 55) was able to make use of the popular hostility to many of the activities of the state, to its bureaucracy and to the continual growth in the burden of taxation. The Tory Party posed as the champion of individual liberty against the state, proposing to cut down taxation, encourage personal initiatives, and reduce the role of government. The Tories were therefore aiming to appropriate popular sentiments of resentment against bureaucratic injustices and inefficiencies, and integrate these sentiments into an ideological system centred on the virtues of private enterprise.

Two important points arise out of the principle that a class advancing towards hegemony needs to build up an ideological system which can act as cement to bind together and unify a bloc of social forces.

First, a class does not achieve hegemony by simply imposing its own outlook on all other classes and social groups. It is necessary to reiterate this point because Gramsci's concept of hegemony has often been thought to consist precisely in the imposition of a class ideology on other classes. On the contrary, the tendency to reduce ideology to the instrument of a class amounts to the economism to which Gramsci was so strongly opposed.

Second, a new ideological system cannot be produced readymade as a kind of intellectual construction worked out by the leaders of a political party. Rather, it has to be put together and gradually built up in the course of political and economic struggles, and its character will depend on the relation of forces existing during the period when it is being constructed. This is one aspect of the revolutionary strategy which Gramsci called a *war of position*, in the course of which the working class builds up a bloc of social forces cemented by a common conception of the world, and thus isolates the capitalist class and deprives it of its allies and of the support which it has derived by integrating national-popular themes into its own ideological system.

Common sense

Hitherto ideology has been discussed in its collective sense, as the expression of communal modes of living and acting. What then is the relation between an organic ideology and the individuals who are influenced by it and who contribute towards it? The starting point for Gramsci is what he calls *common sense*, the uncritical and largely unconscious way in which a person perceives the world; and he said 'all men are philosophers' for all men and women have some conception of the world, or world outlook. Their conscious conception of the world, their religion or ideology, may often be in contradiction with their political activity which can be in advance of their conscious ideas. Thus a person can be said to have two theoretical consciousnesses, 'one which is implicit in his activity and which in reality unites him with all his fellow workers in the practical transformation of the real world; and one, superficially explicit or verbal, which he has inherited from the past and uncritically absorbed' (SPN 333).

It is through common sense that the workers, trying to live their lives under capitalism, have organised their experience. Common sense is the site on which the dominant ideology is constructed, but it is also the site of resistance and challenge to this ideology. Gramsci stresses that the consent which is secured by the hegemony of the bourgeoisie is an *active* consent, not a passive submission. It is not imposed; rather, it is 'negotiated' by unequal forces in a complex process through which the subordination and the resistance of the workers are created and recreated.

The task for Marxist theory is to be a criticism of common sense, and to enable people to develop its positive nucleus – which Gramsci called *good sense* – into a more coherent outlook. And he emphasised that 'it is not a question of introducing from scratch a scientific form of thought into everyone's life, but of renovating and making critical an already existing activity' (SPN 331). The passages in which Gramsci sets out these views on common sense and philosophy (SPN 323-343 and 419-425) are among the most important in the Prison Notebooks.

Continuity in ideology: the search for the positive

In discussing the nature of ideological struggle we said above that a class advancing towards hegemony does not have to make a clean sweep of the opposing ideological systems; rather, it is a matter of transforming existing ideologies by preserving and rearranging some of the most durable elements in a new system. This sense of continuity with the past was deep-rooted in Gramsci, who was always conscious that revolution is both negation and fulfilment, both destruction and construction. Marxism, he said, 'presupposes all this cultural past: Renaissance and Reformation, German philosophy and the French Revolution, Calvinism and English classical economics, secular liberalism ... Marxism is the crowning point of this entire movement of intellectual and moral reformation' (SPN 395).

Gramsci was a polemical thinker. In his letter of 15 December 1930 to his sister-in-law Tatiana he said: 'My entire intellectual formation was of a polemical nature, so that it is impossible for me to think "disinterestedly" or to study for the sake of studying. Only rarely do I lose myself in a particular train of thought and analyse something for its inherent interest. Usually I have to engage in a dialogue, be dialectical, to arrive at some intellectual stimulation. I once told you how I hate tossing stones into the dark. I need an interlocutor, a concrete adversary; even in a family situation, I have to create a dialogue.'[20] But in criticising the ideas of his opponents Gramsci was always engaged in a search for the positive. As Togliatti says 'there is always an awareness that the opposing position ... is part of a much more complex reality than can be revealed by arguments and words, and that one must direct oneself to the study of that reality.'[21] In a note on scientific discussions Gramsci writes:

In the formulation of historico-critical problems it is wrong to conceive of scientific discussion as a process at law in which there is an accused and a public prosecutor whose duty it is to demonstrate that the accused is guilty and has to be put out of circulation. In scientific discussion ... the person who shows himself most "advanced" is the one who takes up the point of view that his adversary may well be expressing a need which should be incorporated, if only as a subordinate aspect, in his own construction. To understand and to evaluate realistically one's adversary's position and his reasons ... means taking up a point of view that is "critical", which for the purpose of scientific research is the only fertile one' (SPN 343-4).

Gramsci applied these principles in his criticism of Benedetto Croce, the outstanding Italian liberal intellectual whose writings on philosophy, history, aesthetics and other subjects exercised a wide influence in Italy, and indeed in Western Europe, in the early years of the century. Gramsci saw him as the leading spokesman of Italian liberalism, and two of the longest series of notes in the Prison Notebooks are devoted to a thorough analysis of Croce's thought and of the role he played in Italian society[22]. In spite of his opposition to Croce's philosophical and political views, which were idealist and profoundly anti-Marxist, Gramsci found a number of positive elements in his thought, especially his concept of 'ethical-political' history which contributed to the development of Gramsci's own concept of hegemony.

The great importance of assimilating the cultural achievements of past generations is stressed by Gramsci in his note on the 'old primary school' entitled 'In search of the educational principle'. In explaining the advantages gained from the study of Latin and Greek, he says: 'Individual facts were not learned for an immediate practical or professional end. The end seemed disinterested, because the real interest was the interior development of personality, the formation of character by means of the absorption and assimilation of the whole cultural past of modern European civilisation (SPN 37).

In his study of Gramsci, James Joll comments on his great range of interests, the extraordinary breadth of his reading and of his historical and philosophical culture; and on the way that he remained rooted in the Italian and European idealist cultural tradition, however much he reacted against figures like Hegel and Croce. Because of this, Joll says that 'it is easier for the non-Marxist to conduct a dialogue with Gramsci than with any other Marxist writer of the twentieth century'.[23]

We have now considered the three main aspects of Gramsci's theory of ideology – its materiality, its role as cement in binding together a bloc of diverse social forces, and its relation to the common sense of individuals; and we have noted Gramsci's understanding of Marxism as the crowning point of the entire cultural movement of the past and his belief that, when criticising one's opponents in the course of ideological struggle, one should also engage in a continual search for the positive.

9   Civil Society, the State and the Nature of Power

Civil society

Previous chapters have examined the relations of classes and social forces and the nature of the political and ideological struggles in which they engage. But we have not yet discussed the state which profoundly affects, and is affected by, the relations of forces (except on p. 16 where Lenin's theory of the state was briefly discussed). It was suggested that his definition of the state as 'an instrument of the ruling class' and as 'a machine for the repression of one class by another' was defective and 'economistic' because it assumed a mechanical relationship between economics and politics or, to be more precise, between the relations of production and the state. We can say that it is an example of a particular form of economism which has persisted long after some of the cruder forms have passed away, and which can be termed 'class reductionism', the tendency to reduce complex political and ideological relations to class relations.

As Gramsci says, 'the historical unity of the ruling class is realised in the state'. Yet the state is also affected by class struggles and by popular-democratic struggles; so that, as Gramsci puts it in the note on the relations of forces discussed earlier (p. 31), the life of the state is 'a continuous process of formation and superseding of unstable equilibria'. Thus, although a hegemonic class predominates in the state, it cannot use the state simply to impose its interests on other classes. The life of the state has a 'relative autonomy' from the ruling class, because it is the outcome of the balance of forces, Gramsci did not employ the term 'relative autonomy' which has come into use since his time, but it expresses very well his own thinking on the state.

The central problem concerning the state is the nature of the power exercised by a ruling class over other classes. For the character of the revolutionary strategy which is appropriate for a class aiming to achieve state power will depend on the understanding reached by that class on the nature of power – what it is and how it is exercised. As Gramsci said 'little understanding of the state means little class consciousness'.

The main proposition advanced by Gramsci is that the state cannot be understood without a thorough understanding of *civil society*. Anyone who reads through the passages in the *Selected Prison Notebooks* collected by the editors under the heading 'state and civil society' is likely to find them very stimulating but also rather confusing. They were written at different times and Gramsci never had the opportunity to put them into a coherent shape. This sense of confusion is heightened by the central role Gramsci gives to *civil society* (contrasted with *political society*) which is difficult to understand because it is never clearly defined. The nearest he comes to a definition is a passage in the note on the formation of intellectuals;

> What we can do, for the moment, is to fix two major superstructural 'levels': the one that can be called 'civil society', that is, the ensemble of organisms commonly called 'private', and that of 'political society' or 'the state'. These two levels correspond on the one hand to the functions of 'hegemony' which the dominant group exercises throughout society and on the other hand to that of 'direct domination' or command exercised through the state and 'juridical' government (SPN 12).

And in his letter of 7 September 1931, he refers to civil society as comprising 'the so-called private' organisations like the church, the trade unions, the schools, etc., and adds 'it is precisely in civil society that intellectuals operate specially ...' (SPN 56n).

Making use of these and other passages in the Prison

Notebooks a definition of civil society can be constructed. It comprises all the 'so-called private' organisations such as churches, trade unions, political parties and cultural associations which are distinct from the process of production *and* from the coercive apparatuses of the state. All the organisations which make up civil society are the result of a complex network of social practices and social relations, including the struggle between the two fundamental classes, capital and labour. One set of institutions, the apparatuses which make up the state, are separated from the organisations of civil society in having a monopoly of coercion. Thus a capitalist society is composed of three sets of social relations: the relations of production, the basic relation between labour and capital; the coercive relations which characterise the state; and all other social relations which make up civil society.

Civil society is the sphere where capitalists, workers and others engage in political and ideological stuggles and where political parties, trade unions, religious bodies and a great variety of other organisations come into existence. It is not only the sphere of class struggles; it is also the sphere of all the popular-democratic struggles which arise out of the different ways in which people are grouped together – by sex, race, generation, local community, region, nation and so on. Thus it is in civil society that the struggle for hegemony between the two fundamental classes takes place. In several passages in the Prison Notebooks Gramsci says that civil society is ethical or moral society, because it is in civil society that the hegemony of the dominant class has been built up by means of political and ideological struggles.

Since civil society includes all the organisations and institutions outside production and the state, it includes the family. The family occupies a distinctive position within civil society, for it is in the family household that women are primarily employed in performing domestic labour and in reproducing, economically and biologically, the commodity labour-power. There is no space here to give adequate consideration to the nature of the very complex system of oppression of women that arises from their performance of unpaid domestic labour. Perhaps it is sufficient at this point to note that this system of oppression is quite different from the system of exploitation of labour by capital, so that womens' struggles against their oppression have a different character from class struggles; the womens' movement in all its variety is therefore a vital component of the bloc of social forces which has to be built up by the working class in its struggle for hegemony.

Gramsci uses the term *political society* for the coercive relations which are materialised in the various institutions of the state – the armed forces, police, law courts and prisons together with all the administrative departments concerning taxation, finance, trade, industry, social security, etc., which depend in the last resort for their effectiveness on the state's monopoly of coercion. He was of course very well aware that the activities of the state are far more than coercion, and that the state apparatuses play a vital part in the organisation of consent; he refers to the 'educative and formative role of the state' (SPN 246). The term 'political society' is not a substitute for the term 'state', but refers only to the coercive relations embodied in the state apparatuses.

Gramsci derived the terms civil society and political society from Hegel, whom he had studied just as Marx and Engels had; and he transformed Hegel's concepts of civil and political society just as Marx and Engels transformed other Hegelian concepts. In Hegel's system, civil society was used to designate the sphere of economic relations, which was indeed the sense in which it was widely used in Britain and France in the eighteenth century; and this was also the sense in which it was used by Marx in his early works, but in the later works of Marx and Engels, after they had developed the theory of historical materialism and the concepts of forces and relations of production, they abandoned the term civil society. It is therefore perfectly legitimate for Gramsci to give a new meaning to a term that has become obsolete, even though it takes a little getting used to in Britain, where the term 'civil servant' is used for officials in the service of the state.

One final point needs to be made before concluding this section on the definition of civil society. One should not think of the distinction between civil society and the state as though they are physically divided into separate areas with a clearly defined boundary between them. They are each composed basically of social relationships, which are coercive in the case of the state, embodied in a great variety of organisations. Hence it is possible for an organisation to embody relations belonging both to civil society and the state. This applies especially to schools, universities and other educational institutions. Gramsci specifically mentions schools as one of the organisations of civil society, because the educational relationship between teacher and student is mainly a non-coercive one. But there are significant elements of coercion involved in education, arising from the need to make attendance at schools compulsory, and the need to rely on taxation to provide the necessary funds. So in most countries schools are provided mainly by the state and they appear, if they are conceived simply as institutions, to form part of the state. But once it is accepted that there can be a certain interpenetration between the relations of civil society and the state, it is possible to explain the paradox that schools belong mainly to civil society even though they are mostly provided by the state.

The integral state

Having defined civil society Gramsci makes his major theoretical proposition. He suggests that 'by state should be understood as well as government apparatus, also the private apparatuses of hegemony' (SPN 261) and elsewhere he writes that the state is 'the entire complex of practical and theoretical activities with which the ruling class not only maintains its dominance but manages to win the consent of those over whom it rules' (SPN 244). This view is summed up in the statement that the state is 'political society plus civil society, in other words, hegemony protected by the armour of coercion' (SPN 262). Gramsci calls this the *integral state* as opposed to the state in the ordinary sense, which he sometimes calls 'the state-as-government' (*stato-governo*) and which he also terms 'political society'.

This approach is bound to seem confusing at first sight. What is the point of taking so much trouble to distinguish between civil society (the sphere of hegemony) and the state (sphere of coercion) and then lumping them both together in the integral state? But the difficulty is solely caused by Gramsci's peculiar terminology: he is using the term 'state' both in its ordinary sense and in the sense of *power*. What he wants to suggest is that the social relationships of civil society are relations of power just as much (though in a different way) as are the coercive relations of the state. A hegemonic class exercises power over subordinate classes in civil society in addition to the state power which it exercises through its predominance in the state. Power is diffused through civil society as well as being embodied in the coercive apparatuses of the state. Thus Gramsci is proposing a far-reaching modification of the classical Marxist theory of the nature of power.

The nature of power

Classical Marxism, including Leninism, takes the view that power is concentrated in the state and is under the exclusive control of the capitalist class (or of a part of that class). The aim of revolutionary strategy is the capture of power. Only *after* the capture of power by the working class can the construction of socialism begin.

This view was powerfully reinforced by the course of the Russian Revolution and was stressed by Lenin in many of his writings, of which *State and Revolution* is the most famous. This theory of power was symbolised by the storming of the Winter Palace in November 1917. The next day at the Congress of Soviets Lenin declared: 'We shall now proceed to construct the socialist order'. The conviction that state power could only be captured by means of a violent insurrection, as in 1917, was abandoned by many communist parties after the Second

World War. The programme of the Communist Party of Great Britain, *The British Road to Socialism* adopted in 1951, declared that it was possible to advance to socialism in Britain, with our long parliamentary traditions, without insurrection on the Soviet model. State power in Britain could be captured peacefully as a result of a parliamentary election which would be the crowning point of a broad mass movement led by the working class. This was a most significant development in revolutionary strategy. But the theory about the nature of power remained the same as before. It was still conceived as located in the state, even though it could be captured by peaceful, parliamentary methods rather than violent, insurrectionary ones. The construction of socialism would only begin after a socialist goverment had been elected.

Gramsci's concept of integral state points in a different direction. Power is conceived as a relation. The social relations of civil society are also relations of power, which are embodied in the great variety of organisations making up civil society, as well as in the state apparatuses. This approach brings out the importance of the relations of forces examined in Chapter 3, where it was shown that civil society consists of a complex network of relations of social forces dominated by the central conflict between capital and labour. The set of apparatuses which make up the state, with its monopoly of coercion, is the principal embodiment (condensation) of these complex relations of forces. But there are other forms of oppression in civil society which are different from the exploitation of labour by capital. There are local, regional, racial, bureaucratic and other forms of domination in which a certain power is exercised and is given a material form in organisations and institutions of one kind or another. Thus the oppression of women is embodied in a complex way in the family as well as other organisations associated with it. This approach, that power is understood as a relationship, has been developed by the French writer Michel Foucault who argues that power is scattered among a great variety of relationships. His work is concerned with the relation of knowledge to power and with the historical emergence of certain techniques or disciplines – natural science, grammar, law, medicine and psychiatry – and the way in which these are converted into relations of power. One can think, for example, of the power exercised by the medical profession within the National Health Service, and of the power wielded by the mass media, etc.[24]

War of position

Wherever there is power there arises resistance to it. The social relations of civil society have therefore given rise, not only to class struggles, but also to the variety of social movements engaging in popular-democratic struggles which do not have a class character, which were the subject of Chapter 5. These struggles affect the nature and the form of the state insititutions and of the organisations of civil society, with the result that these are not mere instruments of the ruling class; rather, they reflect the balance of forces within civil society. In the passage in the Prison Notebooks quoted in Chapter 2 (p. 27), Gramsci compares the organisations of civil society to a powerful system of 'fortresses and earthworks' standing behind the state. In Russia in 1917, where civil society was 'primordial and gelatinous', a frontal attack on the state, which he calls a 'war of movement', could succeed. But in advanced capitalist societies where civil society is highly developed, a different strategy is required – a war of position. The working class has to dismantle the system of fortresses and earthworks supporting the hegemony of the bourgeoisie by building alliances with all the social movements which are striving to transform the relationships within civil society. The hegemonic power exercised by the bourgeoisie through the organisations of civil society has to be increasingly undermined by the countervailing power of the social movements based on the growing activity of the members of these movements, linked together under the leadership of the working class.

The process of revolutionary change from capitalism to socialism consists therefore in the transformation of the social relations of civil society, as the basis for the transformation of the state apparatuses and of the organisations of civil society – churches, schools, political parties, trade unions, etc., as well as the family. This war of position does not exclude the possibility of very sharp struggles, even violent ones, against the coercive organs of the state. What it means is that the decisive struggle for state power can only be won on the basis of a decisive shift in the balance of forces in civil society; and once such a shift has taken place, the opportunities for violent counter-revolutionary attacks from the right will be greatly restricted and will ultimately fail even if they do take place (the problem of violent counter-revolution is further discussed on p. 112).

The shift in the balance of forces and the transformation of the state are likely to take place in stages, so that the achievement of each stage creates the conditions for further advances. The concept of socialist revolution as a process involving stages did not originate with Gramsci. The strategy of the Bolsheviks in the years 1904-7, as set out in Lenin's *Two Tactics of Social Democracy in the Democratic Revolution* (1905) was based on a clear distinction between the democratic and the socialist phases of the revolution. In the democratic phase, the political objective was a radical agrarian reform, an anti-feudal revolution, to destroy the economic power of the landed aristocracy. The democratic revolution would be a bourgeois revolution, clearing the way for the development of capitalism, but would also be a democratic revolution carried out under the leadership of the working class in alliance with the peasantry; and it was expressed in the slogan 'the revolutionary democratic dictatorship of the proletariat and the peasantry.' Lenin's vision of a democratic phase, followed by a socialist phase, did not come to pass owing to the defeat of the 1905 revolution; and in 1917 the conditions were quite different.

The idea of distinct stages arose again at the Seventh Congress of the Comintern in 1935 (referred to on p. 16). The report by Dimitrov discussed the possibility of communists taking part in a united front goverment.[24a] Shortly

after, a people's front government came into being in the
shape of the Spanish Republican Government, which was
described by Dimitrov and other communist leaders as a
'democratic state of a new type'.

In September 1936 Dimitrov said that the Spanish Republic
for which the people were fighting 'will not yet be a Soviet
state, but it will be an anti-fascist left-wing state, participated
in by the genuine left elements of the bourgeoisie ... It is here a
question of organising production without doing away
altogether with private capitalist property ... with the
participation and under the control of the working class and
its allies ... namely, the petty bourgeoisie and the peasantry.'
And he added, in an allusion to the 1905 revolution in Russia:
'Theoretically this may perhaps be correctly expressed as a
special form of the democratic dictatorship of the working
class and peasantry.'[24b] And at the 1937 Congress of the
British Communist Party J.R.Campbell, arguing against the
Trotskyists in Britain and Spain who demanded the
overthrow of the Spanish Republican Government, said that
the only basis for anti-fascist unity was the defence of the
Republic, which was a 'democratic republic of a new type';
it had already given the land to the peasants, the great
newspapers and the radio were in the hands of the working
class, and large-scale industry had been nationalised for the
successful prosecution of the war.[24c] This approach was
developed in the writings of Gramsci's colleague Togliatti,
who had played a leading part in the Seventh Congress. For
Togliatti, the Spanish Republic was the highest point then
achieved by the revolutionary movement in the West; it was
based on a broad alliance which was popular, national and
anti-fascist, and was an intermediate form of democratic state
which, had it emerged victorious, would have facilitated
further transformations in the direction of socialism.[24d]

Thus the socialist revolution was already beginning to be
understood in the international communist movement as a
process involving successive stages, quite independently from
the ideas which Gramsci had set down in his Notebooks,
which had not then been published. Through his concepts of

hegemony and civil society, he added a new dimension to Marxism which provided the theoretical basis for understanding the nature of the transition to socialism, and for developing the appropriate strategy for achieving it.

Towards a communist society

Once the working class has gained state power and taken the principal means of production into public ownership, the transition towards a communist society can begin. The socialist principle 'from each according to ability; to each according to work' creates the conditions for the advance towards a communist society based on the principle 'from each according to ability; to each according to needs'. This will be a classless society which is free from exploitation; it will require an abundance of goods to satisfy the needs of all, a new outlook of cooperation and concern for the common good, and the ending of the division between mental and manual labour.

The contrast between civil society, with its voluntary, autonomous organisations, and the state institutions with their coercive character, enables Gramsci to give a perspective for the development of a socialist society into a communist one. He says that 'it is possible to imagine the coercive element of the state withering away by degrees, as ever more conspicuous elements of civil society make their appearance' (SPN 263). The evolution towards communism consists, then, in the continual extension of civil society and its relations of autonomy, self-government and self-discipline, along with the gradual disappearance of the coercive, hierarchical and bureaucratic elements of the state.

Gramsci recognised that where the working class achieves state power in a backward country without a well-developed civil society, there would have to be an initial period of heavy reliance on the state. He called this a period of *statolatry*, by which he meant very much the same as the term *statism* which has come into use in recent years. This period of statolatry, he says in the note on this subject (SPN 268), is necessary in order to construct a complex and well-articulated civil society in which the individual can govern himself, but which it was not possible to create before the revolution. But he immediately goes on to qualify this statement: 'However, this kind of "statolatry" must not be abandoned to itself, must not, especially, become theoretical fanaticism or be conceived of as "perpetual".' It must be criticised, precisely in order to develop and produce new forms of civil society, in which the initiative of individuals and groups will flourish.

This note on statolatry is valuable for analysing the Soviet Union. The period of statolatry has been exceptionally prolonged and has not been used to develop a 'complex and well-articulated civil society'. Instead, many elements of civil society which existed in Lenin's time were eliminated under Stalin and the system of single-party domination over all spheres of life has proved to possess remarkable durability, not only in the Soviet Union but also in the other Eastern European countries to which it was transferred after the Second World War. Nevertheless, in Czechoslovakia in 1968, and in Poland in 1980-81, powerful movements have arisen towards a pluralist society with a diversity of organisations representing the working class – movements towards a complex and well-articulated civil society. There can be little doubt that a similar development must eventually take place in the Soviet Union, even though the period of statolatry may be exceptionally prolonged.

It may seem contradictory that the transition to socialism in the Soviet Union should have taken the form mainly of a revolution from above, carried out through the agency of the state; it has taken the form of a *passive revolution*, which Gramsci maintains is the strategy employed by the bourgeoisie, whereas the appropriate strategy for the working class is an anti-passive revolution (Chapter 6). But this is not as paradoxical as it seems. It means that the leadership of the Soviet Communist Party under Stalin and his successors adopted and continue to adopt bourgeois political practices inherited from Tsarist Russia. This is not the place to discuss why this has happened, except to suggest that the causes have to be sought in the extreme backwardness of Tsarist society, the exceptionally difficult conditions in which the new Soviet state was born (civil war, invasion, famine, etc.) and the serious defects in the Marxist theory of politics.

Thus Gramsci's theory of civil society and its complex relations with the state provide a perspective for the transition from capitalism to socialism and an understanding of the nature of the revolutionary process. The nature of revolutionary strategy and the role of a revolutionary party will be taken up again in the last two chapters.

10   The Factory Councils' Movement

L'Ordine Nuovo *and the factory councils*

A class which is advancing towards hegemony must strive for leadership in the sphere of production: 'Though hegemony is ethical-political, it must also be economic, founded on the decisive function of the leading group in the decisive sectors of production' (SPN 161). As Gramsci had said in an article written in July 1920, a socialist revolution has to be founded on 'the patient and methodical work needed to build a new order in the relations of production' (SPW I 305).

The practical origin of the concept of hegemony was the factory councils' movement which arose in Turin during the great revolutionary upsurge in Italy in 1919-20. The weekly journal which was founded in May 1919 by Gramsci and his friends Togliatti, Tasca and Terracini, entitled *L'Ordine Nuovo* (The New Order) became the organ of the factory councils. Searching for something in Italy which could play the role which had been played by the soviets in the Russian Revolution, Gramsci and his colleagues seized on the internal commissions in the factories as potential organs of working-class power.

The internal commissions were committees elected by trade union members having limited functions for dealing with grievances, originally very much under the control of the union officials, but towards the end of the war they were becoming a focus for the discontent of the militants with the union leadership. In June 1919 *L'Ordine Nuovo* published an article by Gramsci and Togliatti calling for the transformation of the internal commissions into 'organs of proletarian power, replacing the capitalist in all his useful functions of management and administration'; creating a new system of workers' democracy which would be a school of political and administrative experience and thus effecting a radical transformation of the workers' consciousness. This call met with an immediate response, and the internal commissions developed into factory councils which, building on the revolutionary spirit of the Turin workers, rapidly grew into a powerful movement.

Although the factory councils were inspired by the October Revolution, they were quite different from the Russian soviets. They were a creative application to Italian conditions of the experiences of the Russian workers, not a mechanical copy of the Russian model. They were factory-based organisations for exercising workers' control over production and the labour process, not territorial organisations based on towns and villages and composed of deputies of workers, peasants and soldiers. They drew also on the experiences of British shop-stewards' committees, but differed from them too; the factory councils were to be organs of the workers as producers rather than as wage earners, and all workers participated whether or not they belonged to a trade union.

In September 1920 the post-war revolutionary wave in Italy culminated in the occupation of the factories which, beginning in Milan, quickly spread throughout the country. Inspired by the example of Turin, factory councils sprang up everywhere, and in many factories production continued. Confronted by this immense movement, the leaders of the Italian Socialist Party remained passive, and allowed the reformist CGT leaders (the Italian TUC) to reach a compromise with the government and to call off the occupation. While it had demonstrated the great potentialities of the factory councils movement and had revealed the capacity of the working class for industrial leadership, it ended in defeat. The second half of 1920 witnessed both the rise of Mussolini's fascist movement, and preparations for the foundation of the Italian Communist Party which took place in January 1921.

This is not the place to explore all the aspects of the factory councils' movement, which can be studied in Gramsci's own articles in SPW I. Three themes are of particular importance for the development of the concept of hegemony: (1) the factory councils as embryos of a new state, ending the separation between economic and political struggle; (2) welding the present to the future; and (3) workers' control over the labour process.

Embryos of the new state

For Gramsci, at this relatively early stage in his development as a Marxist, the nucleus of Lenin's thought was the dictatorship of the proletariat; that is, revolution was understood not only as destruction but also as the construction of a fundamentally new type of state. It was necessary to adopt a new kind of political practice, as developed by Lenin and the Bolshevik Party, and to break with the entire parliamentary tradition of the Second International. This tradition was characterised by the gulf which separated the parliamentary leaders from the mass of the workers, and by a style of leadership which expected the workers to remain passive while all the decisions and intiative were concentrated at the top. It was basically no different from the practice of the bourgeois political parties. For Gramsci, following Lenin, the factory councils like the soviets were a new kind of state institution which transformed the relation between leaders and led because they enabled the workers to participate actively in the construction of the new state. The factory councils were an embryonic apparatus of power destined to replace the bourgeois parliamentary state by a system of direct democracy founded on the participation of the masses.

Welding the present to the future

Gramsci's attitude to parliamentary democracy will be considered again in Chapter 13. The second great theme of the factory councils' movement was that the revolution consisted just as much in constructing the new order as in destroying the old one, and that the two processes could take place at the same time. The factory councils were new, socialist organs of power which were developing within the framework of the Italian capitalist state. As Gramsci said: 'How can the present be welded to the future, so that while satisfying the urgent necessities of the one we may work effectively to create and "anticipate" the other?' (SPW I 65). Gramsci was already beginning to formulate the principle that the socialist revolution is not simply a dramatic seizure of state power, to be followed by the construction of socialism, but is a process which begins under capitalism – the principle that was later to be elaborated in the Prison Notebooks into the concept of a war of position.

Taking control of the labour process

Third, the factory councils' movement embodied the principle that the workers should take the control of the labour process out of the hands of the capitalist owners, establishing their leadership in the sphere of production and 'replacing the capitalist in all his useful functions of management and administration'. The workers acted in their capacity as producers, not as wage earners. The factory councils' movement was a 'true school for developing the reconstructive capacities of the workers':

> The working masses must take adequate measures to acquire complete self-government, and the first step along this road consists in disciplining themselves, inside the work-shop, in the strictest possible, yet autonomous, spontaneous and unconstrained manner. Nor can it be denied that the discipline which will be established along with the new system will lead to an improvement in production – but this is nothing but the confirmation of one of the theses of socialism: the more the productive human forces acquire consciousness, liberate themselves and freely organize themselves by emancipating themselves from the slavery to which capitalism would have liked

to condemn them forever, the better does their mode of utilization become – a man will always work better than a slave. So to those who object that by this method we are collaborating with our opponents, with the owners of the factories, we reply that on the contrary this is the only means of letting them know in concrete terms that the end of their domination is at hand, since the working class is now aware of the possibility of *doing things itself*, and doing them well. Indeed from one day to the next it is acquiring an ever clearer certainty that it alone can save the entire world from ruin and desolation (SPW I 95).

Thus the factory councils were the means through which the workers could acquire self-discipline, autonomy, and political consciousness – qualities which were needed for the exercise of national leadership in the sphere of production. As Gramsci put it, 'the era of the active intervention of the labour force in the fields of technique and discipline had begun, and the working class was beginning to acquire the mentality of a ruling class'. New methods of work and new technical developments do not have to be everlastingly identified with the interests of capital. The unity between technical developments and the interests of the capitalist class should be conceived as transitory, as a historical phase of industrial development which is coming to an end. This unity can be dissolved, and technical developments can be conceived, not merely separately from the interests of the ruling class, but in relation to the interests of the working class. The rise of the factory councils' movement was a compelling proof that such a new synthesis was historically mature; it was a demonstration of the new political consciousness which the Turin workers were in the process of acquiring (SPN 202).

In the Prison Notebooks, Gramsci returned to this question in a series of notes collected under the title of 'Americanism and Fordism', where he considers the new forms of organisation and rationalisation of production, which were typified at that time by the 'mass production' and high wages system developed by Ford. Owing to the special conditions which existed in the United States, it was relatively easier than in Europe 'to rationalise production by a skilful combination of force (destruction of trade unionism) and persuasion (high wages, various social benefits, extremely subtle ideological and political propaganda) and thus succeed in making the whole life of the nation revolve around production'. So Gramsci concluded that 'hegemony here is born in the factory'.

Fordism, as Gramsci understood it, was not only concerned with introducing new methods of scientific management for the control of the work process. It also aimed to develop a new type of worker suited to the new type of work. As examples of this Gramsci examines the moral coercion on the workers which was exercised by means of 'prohibition' (banning of all alcoholic drink) and by the concern shown by some American industrialists to regulate and rationalise the sexual affairs and family arrangements of their employees.

> People who laugh at these initiatives (failures though they were) and see in them only a hypocritical manifestation of 'puritanism' thereby deny themselves any possibility of understanding the importance, significance and objective import of the American phenomenon, which is *also* the biggest collective effort to date to create, with unprecedented speed, and with a consciousness of purpose unmatched in history, a new type of worker and of man (SPN 302).

Thus 'the new methods of work are inseparable from a specific mode of life, a specific way of thinking and feeling'.

In other words, ideology plays a crucial role in the capitalist control of the labour process, for ideology as Gramsci conceives it, embodies rules of practical conduct and moral behaviour. For the working class to wrest control of the labour process out of the hands of the capitalists, ideological and political struggle are necessary. The conflicts in the workplace between capitalist management and the workers on issues, such as the terms on which new technology is introduced, are not to be understood as purely economic; they also involve ideological and political struggles. Thus the social relations of civil society penetrate profoundly into the relations of production. Two observations can be made about this.

First, the classical Marxist distinction between economic structure or base, and the political and ideological superstructure, is no longer satisfactory as a way of thinking about society or as an explanation of how social changes take place. It is misleading to think in terms of a sharp separation between a sphere of economics, and a sphere of politics, once it is accepted that the political relations of civil society penetrate into the relations of production. Even more important, the metaphor of base and superstructure implies that changes in the economic structure are the primary cause of changes in politics and ideology, whereas the whole direction of Gramsci's thought, in line with Lenin's, is to attribute revolutionary change to political action; and to establish the principle of the primacy of politics. Although the Prison Notebooks contain many references to base and superstructure, this is in effect replaced in Gramsci's thought by his concept of *historic bloc* to indicate the way in which a hegemonic class combines the leadership of a bloc of social forces in civil society with its leadership in the sphere of production. The process of revolutionary change consists in the disintegration of the historic bloc constructed by the capitalist class and its replacement by a new historic bloc built up by the working class. The primacy of politics, conceived in this way, does not conflict with the basic principle of historical materialism as stated by Marx in the 1859 *Preface to the Critique of Political Economy*: 'The mode of production of material life conditions the social, political and intellectual life process in general.'

Second, in considering the advance from capitalism to socialism it is essential to keep in mind the two distinct elements that characterise the relation between capital and labour. On the one hand, the ownership of capital enables the capitalist to appropriate the surplus labour created by the worker; this is expressed by the relation between profits and wages. On the other hand, the worker is subordinated to the capitalist in the labour process, and it is through this control that capital constantly revolutionises the techniques of production and raises the productivity of the workers. The abolition of the private ownership of the means of production is one aspect of the advance to socialism; the ending of the subordination of the worker in the labour process is the other, in which the arbitrary control by the management in the workplace has to be replaced by the collective control of the workers.

The two elements in the capital-labour relation can be expressed by the distinction between the social and the technical division of labour. The central aspect of the *social* division of labour is the division between the capitalist owners of the means of production and the workers who have only their labour-power to sell. The *technical* division of labour concerns the division between skilled and unskilled workers, between the various skilled occupations such as electrician or engineer, and above all the division between manual and intellectual labour.· The social division of labour can be abolished through the public ownership of the means of production and the creation of some kind of planning system, which can be done in a relatively short period. But the complete overcoming of the technical division of labour, and especially of the division between manual and intellectual labour, is bound to be a prolonged process stretching far into the future. This explains why socialism is a transitional form of society, gradually developing into communism when the antithesis between manual and intellectual labour will have vanished, as Marx outlined in his *Critique of the Gotha Programme.* In *Capital* Marx showed how the skilled craftsman was deprived of his individual control over his own work and was reduced to an appendage of the machine. Under socialism the workers will recover their individuality in an entirely new way as they gradually gain collective control over the labour process.

The crucial point made by Gramsci is that this struggle to wrest control of the labour process away from the capitalist managers begins within capitalism and is an essential part of the struggle for hegemony. The British trade union movement has been built up in the course of struggles, not only for higher wages but also for imposing limits on the arbitrary authority of the capitalists' control of the work process. The insistence by many trade unions on 'mutual agreement' before new work practices are introduced is an example, as also is the making of agreements on the introduction of new technology. These struggles have had successes and have contributed to the strength of the trade unions and their workplace organisation. But up to the present they have been mainly defensive; they have had an economic-corporate, rather than a hegemonic, character. The factory councils' movement was the particular form in which the Turin workers were able, in the conditions prevailing in 1919-20, to mount a challenge to the hegemony of the capitalists in the factory. The very different conditions in Britain in the 1980s will require quite different forms of challenge. Some valuable initiatives have already been taken. These include the work done by the Institute of Workers' Control since its formation in 1968; the action of the shipyard workers who carried the work-in at Upper Clyde Shipbuilders in 1971 to a successful conclusion, inspiring many other actions against redundancy; the movement for workers' cooperatives; the alternative corporate plan worked out by the Lucas Aerospace Shop Stewards' Committee for the manufacture by Lucas of socially useful products instead of destructive weapons, promoting the concept of alternative workers' plans; and the enterprise boards which have been set up by some Labour-controlled local authorities such as the Greater London Council and the West Midlands County Council. The alternative economic strategy of the left, which took shape in the 1970s, has also been a valuable advance and provides a framework for the labour movement to establish its leadership in economic development at national, regional, local and workplace level.

11 Extending the Sphere of Politics

Gramsci's concept of civil society leads in another important direction which has not yet been discussed: it lays the basis for a great extension of the sphere of politics. The organisations which comprise civil society have a great variety of different purposes – political, social, artistic, sporting and so on. What they have in common is that they all embody social practices which are associated with the assumptions and values which people accept, often unconsciously. This is the material aspect of ideology which was discussed in Chapter 5. A ruling class establishes its hegemony by combining these values and assumptions with its own class interests and thus building a social base within civil society for the coercive and administrative power of the state. Thus Gramsci says that hegemony includes the spontaneous consent given by the great masses of the population 'to the general direction imposed on social life by the dominant fundamental class' (SPN 12). If the working class is to advance towards hegemony, it must seek for ways of challenging this spontaneous consent. This can only be done by means of political activity.

Gramsci therefore extends the concept of politics to cover any activities which are intended to change the nature of the spontaneous consent which has been built up in civil society. One of the best illustrations of this conscious extension of political activities is the rise of the women's liberation movement in the 1970s. It has sought to challenge all the values and assumptions which have legitimised a subordinate position for women within the family and society, and thus to stimulate women to think anew for themselves what their role in society should be. In doing this it has built on the feminist movements of the past. In his notes on Americanism and Fordism Gramsci discusses some aspects of the sexual question and in one passage he refers to the need for women to develop a new way of conceiving themselves:

> The formation of a new feminine personality is the most important question of an ethical and civil order connected with the sexual question. Until women can attain not only a genuine independence in relation to men but also a new way of conceiving themselves and their role in sexual relations, the sexual question will remain full of unhealthy characteristics and caution must be exercised in proposals for new legislation (SPN 296).

This extension of the concept of politics, to cover the activity of changing human relationships (and the ideas implicit in them) in all spheres of life, is a most important consequence of the concept of civil society.

For Marx, Engels and Lenin and other Marxist writers before Gramsci, politics was identified with the struggle for state power. The struggles between classes, resulting in continual changes in the state culminating in revolutionary changes, was the substance of politics. State power and political power were interchangeable terms; and the Marxist theory of politics was (and still often is) referred to simply as the Marxist theory of the state. It can certainly be argued that a wider conception of politics is implicit in Marx's thought, especially in his concept of praxis, but it was never made the subject of explicit analysis by him.

If politics is confined to the struggle for state power, it follows that in the transition to communism, when the coercive elements of the state wither away, politics would also wither away; in Engels's famous (though obscure) phrase it would be replaced by the 'administration of things'. For Gramsci, on the other hand (as Eric Hobsbawm has said) politics is the core not only of the strategy for winning socialism, but of socialism itself. Politics extends to embrace a much wider field of human activity than the struggle for state power. Gramsci's view is best set out in the note entitled 'What is man?' (SPN 351-4) and is akin to Aristotle's conception that human beings are fundamentally political by nature. Basing himself on Marx's sixth thesis of Feuerbach that the 'human essence' is the *ensemble* of human relations, Gramsci says that political activity consists in the activity of transforming these human relations, and in doing so one develops one's own capacities and potentialities. (Since he was writing long before the womens' liberation movement, he deserves to be excused for abiding by the convention of his time in using 'man' to include 'woman'):

> So one could say that each one of us changes himself, modifies himself to the extent that he changes the complex relations of which he is the hub. In this sense the real philosopher is, and cannot be other than, the politician, the active man who modifies the environment, understanding by environment the *ensemble* of relations which each of us enters to take part in. If one's own individuality is the *ensemble* of these relations, to create one's own personality means to acquire consciousness of them and to modify one's own personality means to modify the *ensemble* of these relations (SPN 352).

Gramsci took the view that capitalist relations of production were relations which an individual had to enter into independently of his or her will, that is, they were the realm of necessity. Politics, on the other hand, is the activity through which individuals, acting collectively, liberate themselves from necessity. Politics is born on the 'permanent and organic' terrain of economic life but 'transcends it, bringing into play emotions and aspirations in whose incandescent atmosphere calculations involving the individual human life itself obey different laws from those of individual profit, etc.' (SPN 140). Taking part in politics means developing the capacity to think and act for oneself, developing autonomous activity which is not directed from above by external forces. It is linked with the development of one's own conception of the world. Is it better,

Gramsci asks, 'to take part in a conception of the world mechanically imposed by the external environment? Or on the other hand is it better to work out consciously and critically one's own conception of the world and thus, in connection with the labours of one's own brain, choose one's sphere of activity, take an active part in the creation of the history of the world, be one's own guide, refusing to accept passively and supinely from outside the moulding of one's own personality?' (SPN 323).

Thus politics is conceived by Gramsci as a central human activity through which people develop their capacities and potentialities. The transition to socialism requires that civil society should be transformed as more and more people participate actively in this transformation.[25] It is not a question of the gradual disappearance of politics; rather, it has to become a sphere of activity for all, not for the few as at present:

> Marxism is the expression of the subaltern classes who want to educate themselves in the art of government and have an interest in knowing all the truth, even the most unpleasant (Q 1320).

12   The Intellectuals

Definition

The role of intellectuals in capitalist society and in the transition to socialism is a subject which pervades the Prison Notebooks. Indeed, Gramsci attached such importance to it that his original plan for the notebooks was a comprehensive history of the Italian intellectuals. [26] In part, this may have been a reflection of the special conditions in Italy arising from the absence of a unified national state until 1870. This had the result that the Italian language, literature and culture, and the cultural activities of intellectuals, were more important than in other countries. Gramsci took the view that their activities in the centuries before the Risorgimento tended to have a 'cosmopolitan' character on the model of the Roman Catholic Church and to hinder rather than help national unity. The Prison Notebooks are filled with short studies of almost every aspect of intellectual activity in Italy, ranging from popular literature and journalism to works on philosophy, history and economics. In addition to the attention he devotes to Machiavelli, the philosopher Croce and other prominent intellectuals he also examines with care the work of all kinds of minor intellectuals. However, once he had started on the notebooks, the theory of politics and the state, and the concept of hegemony, became his central preoccupation.

Two themes underlie Gramsci's views on intellectuals. First, the need to abolish the division between manual and intellectual labour which has been carried to an extreme under capitalism in the production process, in civil society, and in the state apparatus. Second, the relation between knowledge and power – the nature of the power which is derived from the near-monopoly of knowledge by the ruling class and the need for a fundamental change in the relation between the people and knowledge in the transition to socialism. However, Gramsci does not develop a comprehensive theory of intellectuals; rather, he makes a number of significant observations about their role in society and their relations to the labour movement and to a revolutionary party.

Gramsci's views on intellectuals are set out in the two notes which are placed at the beginning of the Prison Notebooks (SPN 3-23). He rejects what he calls the traditional and vulgarised notion of the intellectual as consisting only of the man of letters, the philosopher and the artist (adding that journalists, who claim to be men of letters and philosophers, also regard themselves as 'true' intellectuals). Intellectuals are not characterised by the intrinsic activity of thinking which is common to all people, but by the function which they perform. 'All men are intellectuals, one could therefore say, but not all men have the function of intellectuals' (SPN 9).

Gramsci therefore extends the definition of intellectuals to all those who have the function of organisers in all spheres of society, in the sphere of production as well as in the spheres of politics and culture. He makes a double break with the habitual notion of intellectuals; they are not only thinkers, writers and artists but also organisers such as civil servants and political leaders, and they not only function in civil society and the state but also in the productive apparatus as engineers, managers and technicians.

His next step is to make a distinction between 'organic' and 'traditional' intellectuals. Every class creates one or more strata of intellectuals 'which give it homogeneity and an awareness of its own function not only in the economic but also in the social and political fields' (SPN 5). The intellectuals do not form a class but each class has its own intellectuals. Thus the capitalists create alongside themselves the industrial managers and technicians, economists, civil servants, and the organisers of a new culture and of a new legal system. Gramsci calls these *organic intellectuals* as distinct from *traditional intellectuals*. Every rising class finds categories of intellectuals already in existence; these traditional intellectuals seem to represent an historical continuity and tend to put themselves forward as autonomous and independent of the ruling class.

Traditional intellectuals

Gramsci argues that 'one of the most important characteristics of any rising class is its struggle to assimilate and conquer "ideologically" the traditional intellectuals'. An example of traditional intellectuals is the ecclesiastics who act as the organic intellectuals of the feudal aristocracy, and were already in existence when the bourgeoisie began its ascent to power. The second example Gramsci gives is the intellectuals of a rural type, the priests, lawyers, teachers, doctors and civil servants who are traditional because they are linked to the peasantry and the small town bourgeoisie, 'not yet elaborated and set in motion by the capitalist system' (SPN 14).

One interpretation of Gramsci's definition would be that traditional intellectuals are those that were the organic intellectuals of a former mode of production which has been superseded – the feudal mode of production – or are the organic intellectuals of a mode of production in course of being superseded – the petty bourgeois mode of production in the Italian countryside in Gramsci's time. It follows that from the point of view of the working class, all the organic intellectuals of the capitalist class are traditional intellectuals. But if this is what Gramsci meant, it seems to me that the term 'traditional' is not very suitable, and in any case it is unnecessary since it adds nothing to the category, already clearly defined, of organic intellectuals of the capitalist class.

An alternative view, taken for example by the editors of the SPN (p. 3) is to seize on Gramsci's remark that traditional intellectuals 'put themselves forward as autonomous and independent of the dominant social group' and define them as 'those whose position in the interstices of society has a certain inter-class aura about it'. But this is a subjective approach, defining a category of people by the notion of themselves that they choose to put forward. Moreover, the notion of class neutrality and autonomy is often held by intellectuals – judges for example – who are certainly performing the function of organic intellectuals of the capitalist class. It seems best, therefore, to accept that Gramsci's category of traditional intellectuals may be very relevant to his analysis of Italian society and Italian history, but is not very appropriate for understanding the role of intellectuals in an advanced capitalist society such as Britain.

Organic intellectuals

In his note on the Risorgimento Gramsci gives the leaders of the Moderate Party as an example of organic intellectuals. The Moderates were 'intellectuals and political organisers, and at the same time company bosses, rich farmers or estate managers, commercial and industrial entrepreneurs, etc.' They realised the identity of the represented and the representative, and formed 'a real, organic vanguard of the upper classes, to which economically they belonged' (SPN 60). Given this organic 'condensation' or concentration they exercised a powerful attraction on the whole mass of intellectuals, such as teachers, who were scattered throughout the Italian peninsula.

The crucial function exercised by the organic intellectuals of the capitalist class is to act as its 'deputies' or agents in organising its hegemony in civil society and its domination through the state apparatus. Gramsci used the word *commessi*, similar to the French *commis* meaning agent or commercial traveller, which he took from Georges Sorel, the principal theorist of French revolutionary syndicalism in the two decades before the first world war. The term *commis* expressed Sorel's anti-intellectualism. He regarded the state as a corps of privileged intellectuals and political parties as being created by politicians to fight for a share in these privileges; politics was nothing but a battle of cliques. The working class movement should exclude intellectuals, and revolution would take the form of a revolution of trade unionists who would organise production without the need for intellectuals or capitalists. Although Gramsci did not share Sorel's anti-intellectual approach or his syndicalist ideas, he found Sorel's intuitions stimulating in developing his own ideas. This applies, not only to intellectuals as *commis* but also to Sorel's notions of 'intellectual and moral reform' and 'historic bloc'.[27]

Gramsci's only concrete analysis of organic intellectuals is the account of the role of the Moderates in the Risorgimento. The Prison Notebooks do not contain any clear account of the organic intellectuals in the Italy of his day or in a modern capitalist society. There are only a number of disconnected statements. He says that in the work of organising hegemony and state domination there develops a whole hierarchy of qualifications and in the state apparatus there exist a series of jobs of an instrumental character. He also refers to complex gradations in the army, ranging from the general staff officers down to the NCOs. It seems likely that if he had made a list of the organic intellectuals of the capitalist class in the 20th century it would have included:

1) In the sphere of production: managers, engineers, technicians, etc.
2) In civil society: politicians, prominent writers and academics, broadcasters, journalists, etc.
3) In the state apparatus: civil servants, officers of the armed forces, judges and magistrates, etc.

However, Gramsci also makes the point that factory technicians do not exercise any political influence over the factory workers; the reverse is the case, and the workers are much more likely to exercise such influence over the technicians. In another passage he refers to the unprecedented expansion of bureaucracy in the modern world. It seems to me that these categories which have increased so greatly in all the advanced capitalist countries – school and university teachers, technicians, scientists and engineers, accountants and subordinate managers, journalists and others in the mass media – do not fit into Gramsci's category of organic intellectuals, and certainly cannot be traditional intellectuals. They are subject to conflicting forces. In so far as they passively carry out the orders of their superiors they are acting as agents of the leading intellectuals and may perhaps be considered to be subordinate organic intellectuals. But in so far as they join trade unions and become drawn towards the labour movement, it makes no sense to describe them as organic to the capitalist class. In addition, many of them are subject to important influences arising from professional traditions. It is surely best to exclude them from the category of organic intellectuals of the capitalist class, and to confine this category to the leading personnel whose links with the ruling class justify the description of organic – writers and academics like the philosopher Croce who exercised a wide influence on behalf of the liberal state in Italy, senior officials in the civil service, the top layer of officers in the armed forces, the judges in the High Court, etc.

If this is right, then we have to accept that Gramsci does not provide a comprehensive theory of intellectuals. The category of organic intellectuals, organisers of hegemony for the two fundamental classes, does not cover the great majority. On the other hand, his claim that all men are intellectuals is too all-embracing. While it may be important from some points of view to stress that all men and women engage in the activity of thinking, the fact is that some have received special training in colleges and other institutions which enables them to acquire special skills related to their function in society. It is this which separates them from the great majority of workers, and gives them professional and corporate interests and traditions. They have been consituted into a variety of 'middle strata' capable of playing a distinctive part in politics which can be very significant indeed. They are therefore a vital component of the broad alliance which has to be built up by the working class if it is to achieve a hegemonic role in society.[28]

Turning now to Gramsci's organic intellectuals, he argues that if the working class is to raise itself from a subaltern class to take over the leadership of the nation, and to acquire the necessary political consciousness through a profound moral and intellectual reform, it must create its own organic intellectuals. Gramsci does not hesitate to use the strong term 'élite' to make clear that people who are specialised in the task of leadership are required:

> Critical self-consciousness means, historically and politically, the creation of an élite of intellectuals. A human mass does not 'distinguish' itself, does not become independent in its own right without, in the widest sense, organising itself; and there is no organisation without intellectuals, that is without organisers and leaders ... But the process of creating intellectuals is long, difficult, full of contradictions, advances and retreats, dispersals and regroupings, in which the loyalty of the masses is often sorely tried (SPN 334).

The new intellectuals required by the working class differ profoundly from the bourgeois intellectuals:

> The mode of being of a new intellectual can no longer consist in eloquence, which is an exterior and momentary mover of feelings and passions, but in active participation in practical life, as constructor, organiser, 'permanent persuader' and not just a simple orator (but superior at the same time to the abstract mathematical spirit) (SPN 10).

Above all, the relationship between a class and its organic intellectuals is different for the capitalist and the working class. Gramsci holds that a revolutionary party must play a key role as an organic intellectual of the working class. Thus every member of the party should be regarded as an intellectual. 'A party might have a greater or lesser proportion of members in the higher grades or the lower, but this is not the point. What matters is the function, which is leading (*direttivo*) and organisational, i.e. educational, i.e. intellectual' (SPN 16). As Togliatti put it in his lecture on Gramsci in 1958, the party should be a 'collective intellectual'.[29]

This does not of course mean that the revolutionary party

should be the only organic intellectual of the working class. Gramsci proposes that every member of the party should be regarded as an organic intellectual, not that every organic intellectual of the working class should be a member of the party. There is clearly a very significant role for intellectuals who adopt a Marxist viewpoint – and there are many varieties of Marxism nowadays – without becoming a member of a revolutionary party. What is important is the nature of their relationship with the people. If they remain in a separate compartment of their own – as armchair Marxists – they are not likely to contribute much to the democratic and labour movement:

> The intellectual's error consists in believing that it is possible to *know* without understanding and especially without feeling and passion ... that the intellectual can be an intellectual ... if he is distinct and detached from the people-nation (*popolo-nazione*) without feeling the elemental passions of the people, understanding them and thus explaining and justifying them in a particular historical situation, connecting them dialectically to the laws of history, to a superior conception of the world ... History and politics cannot be made without passion, without this emotional bond between intellectuals and the people-nation. In the absence of such a bond the relations between intellectuals and people-nation are reduced to contacts of a purely bureaucratic, formal kind; the intellectuals become a caste or a priesthood ...

Although this passage begins by referring to intellectuals as individuals, the mention of bureaucracy indicates that Gramsci is not only thinking of the importance of popular beliefs and of 'common sense' in the work of the intellectuals; he is also thinking of the relations between a revolutionary party (collective intellectual) and the people, and of the danger that the party may lose touch with the masses and become bureaucratic or, as he says elsewhere, 'mummified and anachronistic'. The passage continues:

> If the relations between intellectuals and the people-nation,

between leaders and led, is the result of an organic participation in which feelings and passion become understanding and thence knowledge ... then and then only is the relation one of representation. Only then can there take place an exchange of individual elements between rulers and ruled, leaders and led, that is to say the realisation of a life in common which alone is a social force, only then is the 'historic bloc' created (SPN 418).[30]

Gramsci is here using the term 'historic bloc' in a different sense from his principal meaning (see p. 86) where it concerns the relation between politics and production. His discussion of the proper relation between a revolutionary party and the people and of the dangers of bureaucracy opens up the whole question of the nature and role of the party, which is considered in the final chapter.

13 Revolutionary Strategy

The revolutionary process

Gramsci's strategy of the war of position has been discussed briefly in a number of places already, more particularly on pages 74-76 of Chapter 9. Here I want to bring together the different aspects of the war of position which have been examined, to compare Gramsci's strategy with the approach of social democracy and of leftism, and then to consider the relation between the advance to socialism and parliamentary democracy.

In contrast to classical Marxism which held that power was concentrated in the state, Gramsci holds that power is diffused throughout civil society as well as being embodied in the coercive apparatuses of the state. The struggle of the working class for socialism in Britain cannot be confined to the winning of state power, but has to be concerned with the transformation of the social relations of civil society as well. In the course of the struggles against the forms of oppression within civil society a great variety of social movements have come into being, such as those concerned with women, pensioners, tenants, young people, students; or those based on racial, regional or national minorities; those concerned with peace; the ecological movement concerned with the environment, and so on. These movements are engaged in popular democratic struggles which do not have a purely class character. It is necessary for the working class to achieve hegemony in civil society through building alliances with all these social movements, combining them with the class struggle so as to create a national-popular collective will. Thus the advance to socialism is a process taking place in stages, not a sharp rupture or explosion confined to a single historical moment when the working class seizes state power.

The war of position as conceived by Gramsci is not simply a question of building alliances with existing, fully formed social movements. Instead, the task is to stimulate their development, striving continually to extend the sphere of politics to the whole of society and to create a more complex and mutli-dimensional civil society. The aim of the working class is to bring about a broad democratic alliance: it is broad because its scope needs to be continually extended, and it is democratic because each of the social movements preserves its own autonomy and makes its own specific contribution. It is also democratic because more and more people are drawn in to take an active part in politics and to acquire more control over their own lives. The advance to socialism is a gradual process involving the extension of democratic control over all areas of life; in the course of the struggle to extend democracy more and more people will come to see that the replacement of capitalism by a system of public ownership and socialist planning is a necessary condition for the fullest development of democracy.

Gramsci's war of position is therefore founded on a new conception of democracy. It is important to demand that the limitations of parliamentary democracy must be overcome, by the abolition of the House of Lords and the monarchy, by giving the House of Commons more effective control over the Cabinet and the executive, by the reform of the mass media and by a host of other reforms such as proportional representation. It is also very important to insist that parliamentary democracy needs to be supplemented by a growing variety of forms of direct democracy which enable people to participate in political activities in the local community, and to acquire control over the labour process in the workplace. But it is necessary to go beyond these two demands and to recognise that the growth of the social movements adds a new dimension to traditional conceptions of democracy. It is not enough to accept the need for a plurality of political parties; it is also necessary to recognise that a pluralism of social movements is a condition for a fully developed democracy. The growth of these movements will in turn have important effects on the forms of parliamentary and direct democracy. In the process of building alliances with these movements – creating a new historic bloc – the working class aims at a hegemony based on the recognition that national unity can only be founded on diversity.

So far in this book I have referred simply to 'the working class' as the social force which leads the challenge to the hegemony of the capitalist class. But this is of course a great simplification. The working class, far from being a single monolithic bloc, is very diverse. There are many divisions within it, such as those between skilled and unskilled workers, between manual and non-manual workers, between the employed and the unemployed, between male and female workers and between those who are organised in trade unions and those who are not; and there are important divergencies in politics, religion and culture – the 'common sense' of the British workers, to use Gramsci's term, is very varied. This diversity of outlooks and interests can give rise to sectional struggles which predominate when the working class is in the economic-corporate stage of its development. Chapter 3 examined the need for the working class to transcend the economic-corporate stage through a process of moral and intellectual reform, in which the political consciousness of the workers develops so that the need to take into account the interests of other classes and social movements is more and more understood. These profound changes in political consciousness and political practice can only be achieved under the leadership of a revolutionary political party. Only a political party, comprising the most advanced members of the class, can take the political initiatives which are needed at each stage of the struggle in order to shift the balance of forces in favour of the working class. Before examining Gramsci's views on the role and nature of a revolutionary party in the next chapter, I want to explore the characteristics of the war of

position more fully, by contrasting it with the main alternative
strategies, the social democratic and the leftist.[31]

The social-democratic approach

One of the distinguishing elements of social democracy is its
insistence that the advance to socialism must be gradual and
peaceful and cannot take the form of a violent revolution.
Thus at first sight Gramsci's war of position, stressing that
revolution is a process, might seem to have much in common
with the social-democratic approach. Further thought,
however, shows that this is not the case. Right-wing leaders of
the Labour Party, such as Wilson and Callaghan, have been
inspired mainly by a belief in equality and social justice, to be
achieved by means of reforms which do not end the
domination of capital. Socialism is envisaged as the outcome
of a gradual accumulation of reforms. In practice, as the
difficulties of British capitalism increased, they abandoned
most of the reforms.

Central to the outlook of social democrats is their belief that
these reforms can be handed down from above, through the
agency of the existing state. They are clearly deeply
committed to parliament in the sense that, once they have
been elected, they should be left to get on with the job. The
state is seen as a neutral machine which can be used by a
parliamentary majority without having fundamental changes
made in it. Social democrats are therefore opposed to the
mobilisation of the people to exert pressure through popular
struggles, and to the development of forms of direct
democracy in workplace and community to enable more and
more people to take part in politics. Their opposition to
democratic reforms within the Labour Party is consistent with
this approach. The result is that their social reforms have
tended to strengthen the bureaucratic nature of the state and
its remoteness from the people. The political practice of social
democracy basically conforms with the liberal political
practices within the traditions of British parliamentarism.
The kind of social transformation it envisages can thus be

characterised as a passive revolution in Gramsci's sense.

British social democracy has, moreoever, been deeply committed to 'corporate' forms of representation which have sought to build up a partnership between representatives of capital (through employers' organisations such as the Confederation of British Industry) and of labour (through the TUC and the trade unions) and the state. The development of corporatism after 1910 was discussed in Chapter 7.

The nature of British social democracy can only be grasped through a study of the history of the Labour Party which was brought into existence in 1900 by the trade unions to defend them in parliament against attacks outside it by employers and the law courts. Unlike the continental social democratic parties in Germany, France, Italy and elsewhere, the Labour Party was set up by the trade unions as a defensive act, to represent them in parliament, not to transform society. However, it was also an alliance between trade unionists and socialists, who were organised principally in the Independent Labour Party, and in other affiliated organisations such as the Fabian Society and the Social Democratic Federation (the small Marxist party which disaffiliated in 1902, but affiliated again in 1916 as the British Socialist Party). Thus the party had a 'broad church' quality, embracing a wide range of views from right to left, a quality it still retains. The deeply radicalising effect of the 1914-18 war on the working class had profound effects on the Labour Party. At its 1918 conference it adopted a socialist objective, expressed in the famous clause 4 of its constitution; 'To secure for the workers by hand or by brain the full fruits of their industry and the most equitable distribution thereof that may be possible upon the basis of the common ownership of the means of production, distribution and exchange ...' The 1918 constitution also provided for individual membership of the Labour Party for the first time, thus creating the potential for a mass campaigning party in the localities. However, the social-democratic outlook of Henderson, Macdonald and others ensured that this potentiality was not developed; instead the constituency Labour Parties functioned mainly as electoral machines for organising support at the parliamentary and local elections (though there were exceptions to this, such as the remarkable struggles of the Poplar councillors for the equalisation of the rates, higher poor relief and other measures, under George Lansbury in the 1920s).[32] This electoral approach was reflected in the party constitution which ensured that the Parliamentary Labour Party was effectively independent from the annual conference.

In the late 1960s, however, the deeply disappointing performance of the Labour governments under Harold Wilson (1964-70) began a shift to the left within the Labour Party which was strengthened by the industrial struggles under the Tory Government (1970-74), and further stimulated by the disillusion among the party's rank and file caused by the Labour Governments from 1974-79 under Wilson and Callaghan. Since the late 1960s the campaign for a radical alternative economic strategy, for greater democracy within the Labour Party and for a more participatory style of politics in the constituency Labour Parties gained very significant successes, and loosened the hold of social democracy within the party. This process of democratic renewal in the party is further discussed in Chapter 14.

However, the struggle against social democracy in the Labour Party and the trade unions does not mean that social democrats are to be treated as enemies of the working class and described as 'agents of the bourgoiesie' or by other insulting terms which became widespread among communists in the late 1920s, especially during the sectarian 'class against class' period of 1929-33 (see p. 16 above). On the contrary, it must be recognised that social democracy, although it has lost ground among the active membership of the Labour Party, is still deeply rooted in the British working class. Socialists and communists can find a great variety of issues around which alliances with social democrats can be formed; examples are the defence of democratic rights threatened by Conservative governments, the search for peace, and the work for alternative economic strategies to fight unemployment. The nature of any alliances with social democrats will depend on the political situation and the balance of forces existing at any moment. The test of a successful alliance is the extent to which people are moved into action, so that through their experiences they come to understand that the partial objectives for which they are striving – peace, jobs, democratic rights, etc. – can only be fully achieved through socialism.

This has necessarily been a brief discussion of a very large subject, which has been further complicated by the creation in 1981 of the Social Democratic Party. The term *social democracy* which I have sought to define here is concerned with the ideas and political practices of the right wing in the Labour Party and the trade union movement – an outlook which has also been called *Labourism*. It does not cover the Social Democratic Party, although there is evidently a close relation between the two. The main purpose of this short analysis of British social democracy has been to bring out the fundamental contrast between its approach and the Gramscian war of position.

The leftist approach

The concept of revolution as a process is rejected by the leftists who adhere to the idea of Marxism-Leninism that power is concentrated in the state, and consider that the Russian Revolution of 1917 is the model for a socialist revolution in advanced capitalist societies. They look forward to a period of mounting class struggle leading to a revolutionary situation in which capitalist rule begins to break down, and new revolutionary organs are built up, consisting primarily of factory-based workers' councils. These councils (like the soviets in Russia in 1917) create a situation of 'dual power'. Under the leadership of a revolutionary party the working class seizes state power and the new workers' councils become the foundation of the socialist state. Thus leftists envisage the socialist revolution as an insurrection which takes place at a single historical moment. There are four other main elements in the leftist approach.

1) The leftists operate with a simplified version of society

which is understood almost wholly in terms of the class struggle between capital and labour, and they do not grasp the complexity of civil society where power is diffused in a variety of forms of oppression. They tend therefore to reduce all popular-democratic struggles to class struggles, and hence they do not understand that in building alliances with the peace movement or the women's movement, it is essential to respect and encourage the autonomy of these social movements and to recognise the special contribution they can make to a socialist society. Instead, leftists tend to have an instrumental approach to popular-democratic struggles, that is, they see them as instruments which can be used to further the class struggle. Their attitude to these social movements is therefore liable to be deeply sectarian, inhibiting the building of alliances.

2) Leftists hold that the state is an instrument of the capitalist class and that the task of the working class is to smash it and replace it with an entirely new socialist state. They reject Gramsci's view that the state is the product of the balance of class and social forces in civil society, that it is a vital arena for class and popular-democratic struggles, and that it can be transformed in the course of the revolutionary process into a socialist state. Thus leftists reject the entire system of parliamentary and local government democracy as an instrument of capitalism (as formal democracy), holding that it has to be replaced by workers' councils. But this is a very narrowing vision, for workers' councils based on the workplace exclude millions of people such as housewives, pensioners, the unemployed, the self-employed and workers in small firms. Certainly, direct democracy in the workplace has a vital part to play; and certainly, the British parliamentary system needs far-reaching reform; but they are complementary, not opposed to each other as the leftists consider.

3) Leftists draw a sharp distinction between reform and revolution. Reformist demands are those which can be conceded by the capitalist state without seriously harming

existing property relations and serve to reconcile the working class to continued rule by the capitalists; in contrast there are revolutionary demands which bring the workers into conflict with the capitalists and their state, plunging the system into crisis and demonstrating to the workers that socialism is the only answer. An example of a 'revolutionary' demand is the proposal for the nationalisation of the two hundred largest monopolies and the whole financial sector and the immediate adoption of a system of socialist planning. The difficulty about this type of demand is that a socialist revolution is required for its implementation. It is far in advance of the present level of political consciousness of the British people, and fails to offer any strategy for getting from where we are now to the point where a 'revolutionary situation' comes into being. Leftists also put forward immediate demands, such as the 35-hour-week, but these are not valued mainly for their intrinsic benefits; rather, it is hoped that the struggle to achieve them will raise the revolutionary spirit of the workers and accelerate the crisis of capitalism.

The leftists are right to criticise the kind of reforms which are carried out in such a way as to damp down popular activity, which tend to strengthen the existing state and help to shift the balance of forces to the right – reforms which contribute to a passive revolution. But they are wrong to assume that all reforms necessarily have that character. On the contrary, the campaign for a particular reform and its successful achievement may have a very positive effect; it may move more people into action and raise the level of their political consciousness; it may enhance the democratic control exercised by people over their own lives, and it may help to strengthen the network of alliances between the labour movement and popular-democratic social movements. In short, the successful campaign for a reform may shift the balance of forces in favour of the working class, and help to build up its hegemony.

The role of any particular reform depends on the circumstances. Thus a demand for higher wages for a particular section of workers in an industry – say the skilled workers – could in certain conditions have a divisive effect and result in the strengthening of the employers, or it could serve to arouse a widespread movement of solidarity which would strengthen the trade unions in the industry and even have important political repercussions. The choice of which reforms should have priority at any moment is not at all easy. As Gramsci said: 'Knowing how to find each time the point of progressive equilibrium (in the sense of one's own programme) is the art of the politician ... really of the politician who has a very precise line with a wide perspective of the future' (Q 1825). This is precisely the task which can only be fulfilled by a revolutionary party which should, through its grasp of Marxism, its collective experience and capacity for constructive discussion, and its close links with the people, develop the capacity to take the right political initiatives at the right time.

There are of course a great variety of reforms to be fought for. One distinction has become very important in recent years in Britain. Many reforms consist simply of 'demands for more' of something, such as a demand for higher pay, shorter hours, more public expenditure on housing or health, higher pensions, etc. On the other hand, there are many reforms which are not merely quantitative, but which will also make a qualitative change in social relations. For example, the demand for equal pay is far more than a demand that women who are now doing the same jobs as men should get the same pay. It implies that women should have equal access to all the skilled and better-paid jobs from which they are still largely excluded; it involves a far-reaching change in the nature of the relationships between men and women both at work and in the home – a change which is an integral part of the advance to socialism and can only be brought about through a prolonged political and ideological struggle. In all areas of life it is possible to put forward *alternative plans* which not only improve living conditions but also contribute to transforming social relations in the direction of greater democratic control –

plans which are realistic and capable of being implemented now and which 'weld the present to the future'. This is a central feature of the Gramscian war of position, and distinguishes it clearly from leftism as well as from social democracy.

4) Leftists argue that a gradual, non-violent advance to socialism is impossible, because at a certain stage the ruling class will resort to an armed rebellion against a left-wing government in order to protect its power and privileges before it is too late. This has already been briefly discussed on p. 75. The strategy of the war of position cannot exclude the possibility of attempts at repressive actions by sections of the armed forces. But a strategy which is founded on the concept of hegemony can make it very unlikely that they will take place. What is important is that, if a shift in the balance of forces has brought a left-wing government to power, it should not take measures which are in advance of the level of political consciousness of the majority of the population (it is precisely the leftists who often advocate measures of this kind). Rather, the government should only carry out policies for which it can ensure popular understanding and support. Violent repressive actions by sections of the armed forces or other groups are unlikely to be undertaken unless the right-wing forces have first secured a fair amount of political support. Skilful leadership by the left can avoid this. Opportunities may arise to take advantage of divisions among the capitalist class (between monopoly capital and small business, between the financial and industrial sectors, etc.). Moreover, a shift in the balance of forces in favour of the left will have repercussions inside the armed forces and the police, winning support from the rank and file and among the officers.

Taking all this into account, the deep-rooted belief which the British people have in parliamentary democracy with is great historical traditions, will make it very difficult for any section of the armed forces to gather support for serious repressive action, unless it is undertaken by an adventurist group which will be easily defeated.

Thus the leftist claim that a war of position is bound to be defeated by violent counter-revolution is not justified. If the concept of hegemony is sound, there is no alternative to a war of position – to the building of a broad alliance stage by stage through political and ideological struggle as the basis for the transformation of the state, including its coercive apparatuses.

This analysis of leftism has necessarily been rather abstract, for space does not allow a consideration of the great variety of actual leftist organisations in Britain. They each have their own special features and certainly do not conform exactly to the characteristics set out above. There is in fact a wide range of leftism from the most extreme sectarianism to the very moderate.

Traditional leftism

There is a significant trend in the British labour movement which is quite separate from the more extreme forms of ultra-leftism. This trend is strongly represented, for example, within the British Communist Party and in other West European Communist parties, and has been influential in the French Communist Party in the years following the break with the Socialist Party in 1977. Those who support this trend do not accept the Gramscian concept of hegemony and the importance of popular-democratic struggles. They tend to reduce these to class struggles, and to share the leftist view of the state as an instrument of the capitalist class (or of the monopoly capitalists). In Britain they are fond of stressing two main themes: 'the leading role of the industrial working class' with its great traditions of militant class struggle and trade union organisation; and the necessity for a highly disciplined revolutionary party. But while it is true that socialism cannot be achieved without the decisive support of the organised industrial core of the working class, it is equally true that militant struggles by this key section cannot be sufficient. The industrial working class does not possess a 'leading role' which is conferred on it by virtue of the key position it occupies in the economic structure. On the contrary, it can only win a position of leadership, of hegemony, if it gains an understanding of how to build alliances with other sectors of the population and with social movements which do not arise directly out of class conflict.

Similarly, revolutionary parties can only succeed in unifying a broad democratic alliance if they recognise the autonomy of these social movements. Unity cannot be achieved simply by virtue of a high degree of discipline. It is no accident that those who stress the 'leading role' of the working class and the need for a disciplined party tend also to admire the Soviet Union as the model for socialism for Britain; for it is precisely in the Soviet Union that social unification is imposed in authoritarian style by means of a highly disciplined, centralised Communist Party.

This type of traditional leftism tends also to be distrustful of intellectuals and hence also of the new social movements which developed in the late 1960s, such as Women's Liberation or the ecology movement, in which intellectuals and 'middle strata' played a very prominent part. This had the effect in France that the middle strata (technicians, middle managers, young intellectuals, young farmers) provided the social base for the renewal of the Socialist Party under Mitterand, and were not won over by the French Communist Party, which proved unable to extend its influence widely beyond its traditional manual working class base.[33] In this there is a great contrast with the Italian Communist Party which, in the tradition of Gramsci and Togliatti, has achieved a wide influence among Italian intellectual circles and the middle strata.

Perhaps enough has been said to indicate the profoundly sectarian effect of this type of leftism.

Parliamentary democracy and socialism

This discussion of the war of position, in contrast with the social democratic and leftist approaches, has stressed that an integral aspect of the revolutionary process is the transformation of the state, not its replacement by a system of workers' councils or soviets. However, it must be frankly admitted that in doing so, this book has gone beyond the Prison Notebooks. Gramsci never abandoned his belief in the factory councils as the embryonic apparatus of power, destined to replace the bourgeois parliamentary state by a system of direct democracy which, in his view, would enable the workers to participate actively in the work of administration. His writings on the factory councils in *L'Ordine Nuovo* in 1919-20 were discussed in Chapter 10. In a note written in 1933-34 Gramsci contrasts them favourably with elective parliamentary systems (SPN 192-3). The few other notes where parliamentary democracy is mentioned are consistent with this approach. Thus Gramsci never went beyond the Leninist view that direct democracy based on factory councils should replace parliamentary democracy.

Parliamentary democracy is based on freedom of association and competition between different political parties; it requires a multi-party system. The one-party system which has become characteristic of the Soviet model of socialism is inconsistent with parliamentary democracy. Quintin Hoare, in his introduction to SPW II argues that the acceptance by Gramsci in these years of Soviet reality as a universal model was 'a crucial limitation' to his thought, both before 1926 and afterwards in the Prison Notebooks (p. xviii). But there is surely no justification for this view. While it is true that there is no explicit criticism of the Soviet model in the Prison Notebooks, there is a strong implicit criticism in the passage on statolatry which was discussed on p. 78. Much more important, though, is the point that the use of a single political party to impose unity on all the different classes and social groups in an authoritarian manner is incompatible with Gramsci's concept of hegemony and his strategy for the advance to socialism. His perspective of the revolutionary process as the transition towards a complex and well-articulated civil society is inconceivable without a multi-party system, that is, without the freedom to form political parties and other organisations to represent the different classes, social groups and social movements in society, and to represent the different tendencies within the working class and other classes. As in the case of the transformation of bourgeois parliamentary democracy, Gramsci's concept of hegemony provides the theoretical foundation for a revolutionary strategy which is multi-dimensional and multi-party.

It remains to consider Gramsci's views on the role and character of a revolutionary Marxist party.

14   The Revolutionary Party

Gramsci's views

Gramsci assembled some of his principal notes on politics under the title 'The Modern Prince'. The first note begins with an analysis of *The Prince*, the book which Machiavelli addressed to Lorenzo de Medici, the ruler of Tuscany, in 1515. In it the author discusses what the prince must be like if he is to found a new state. But the real purpose of the book, according to Gramsci, was not to convince the prince, but to convince the Italian people, and to show how they could develop a 'collective will' as the foundation for a nation state of the type which already existed in France and Britain. In order to represent the process whereby a collective will, directed towards a given political objective, is formed, Machiavelli embodied his conception in the person of a prince and represented the process in terms of the qualities and characteristics of a concrete individual. Such a procedure, Gramsci says, stimulated the artistic imagination of those who had to be convinced. The prince was a symbol of an ideal leader, a purely theoretical abstraction. However, in a dramatic moment of great effect in the famous last chapter of the book 'the elements of passion and myth which occur throughout the book are drawn together and brought to life':

> In the conclusion, Machiavelli merges with the people, becomes the people; not, however, some 'generic' people, but the people whom he, Machiavelli, has convinced by the preceding argument – the people whose consciousness and whose expression he becomes and feels himself to be, with whom he feels identified.

The entire 'logical' argument now appears as nothing other than auto-reflection on the part of the people – an inner reasoning worked out in the popular consciousness, whose conclusion is a cry of passionate urgency. The passion, from discussion of itself, becomes once again 'emotion', fever, fanatical desire for action (SPN 126).

This eloquent passage expresses Gramsci's view of politics as an art as well as a science; political and ideological struggle does not only require a cool and scientific analysis of the existing balance of forces; it should also stimulate the imagination, drawing on the cultural heritage of the nation. In the conditions of modern capitalism, the organiser of the national-popular collective will cannot be an individual like Machiavelli's prince; it can only be a political party – and Gramsci gives the title 'The Modern Prince' to his longest series of notes on politics to emphasise the crucial importance of the revolutionary party, which he calls 'the first cell in which there come together the germs of a collective will tending to become universal' (SPN 129).

There are two main issues which are discussed by Gramsci in his writings on the revolutionary party: what should be the relation between the party and the working class, and on what principles should the party be organised? Gramsci's views on these questions were developed in the course of the prolonged struggle which he led from 1923-26 to overcome the leftist influence of Amadeo Bordiga, the founder and first leader of the Italian Communist Party, whose outlook dominated the party in the early years of its existence. He took the view that the Communist Party lived in perpetual danger of being infiltrated by reformist and petty-bourgeois ideas; in order to remain immune from these influences it had to hold itself strictly apart from other political parties and movements, and concentrate on perfecting its organisation and discipline. Then, when the conditions for revolutionary action had matured, it would be able to lead the working class in a successful assault on the capitalist state.

Gramsci argued that this approach was the result of the

economism that was deeply rooted in the Italian labour movement, and had influenced the leaders of the Italian Socialist Party as well as Bordiga. The form taken by this economism was a 'mechanical determinism' which considered that capitalism was developing inexorably towards economic collapse as its internal contradictions became greater. (Economism was discussed in Chapter 1, p. 11). This kind of mechanical determinism tended to promote a passive attitude of waiting for the inevitable economic collapse, and prevented the party from taking political initiatives and developing close links with the workers and peasants and their organisations. During the two years 1924-26 when Gramsci was the general secretary of the party, he and his colleagues in the leadership succeeded in overcoming the influence of the leftists and in winning the majority of party members for Leninist principles, despite the extraodinary difficulties created by the conditions of police persecution and semi-legality in which the party had to work. Gramsci's views on the party are set out in his writings in this period and in particular in the 'Lyons Theses' which were drafted by him and Togliatti and adopted by an overwhelming majority at the third congress of the party held at Lyons in France in January 1926 (SPW 2 364-75).

The 'Leninist principles' for which Gramsci stood were the principles of strategy, tactics and organisation developed by Lenin and the Bolshevik Party and adopted by the Comintern in the 1920s. The Italian Communist Party is seen as the political organisation of revolutionaries, in other words it is the 'vanguard of the proletariat'. Its task is to organise and unify all the forces necessary for the revolution and to lead an 'insurrection' against the bourgeois state and for the foundation of a workers' state. With its strategy and tactics, the party 'leads the working class' in major historical movements and in day-to-day struggles alike. Its members participate in all the organisations in which the working people are assembled, with the aim of winning a majority for Communist leadership.

While the leading bodies of the party are elected, the organisation of the party should be centralised under the leadership of the central committee. 'An iron proletarian discipline must reign in its ranks'. The centralisation and cohesion of the party 'require that there should not exist organised groups within it which take on the character of factions'. Gramsci contrasted the Communist Party with the Italian Socialist Party and other social-democratic parties in which 'factional struggle is the normal method of working out a political orientation and selecting a leading group', and in which much was discussed but little resolved. Instead, the Communist parties choose as the norm of their internal life 'the organic collaboration of all tendencies through participation in all leading bodies'. The organisation of the party is determined by the task confronting it, that of leading an insurrection for the overthrow of the fascist state.

This book has sought to show that in the Prison Notebooks Gramsci developed the Marxist theory of politics well beyond the stage it had reached under Lenin. However, the passages in the Notebooks referring to the revolutionary party and to the relations between party and class do not, it seems to me, show any significant advance on Lenin's ideas. Gramsci remains within the framework of the Leninist principles for which he stood in the years 1923-26.

Perhaps the most significant and often-quoted passages are those on intellectuals, where Gramsci says that the organic intellectuals are the organisers of the hegemony of a class, and that for the working class, every member of the revolutionary party should be regarded as an intellectual. Hence as Togliatti said, the party should be regarded as a 'collective intellectual' (See p. 99 above). This follows from Gramsci's extension of the definition of intellectuals to include those who have the function of organisers in all spheres of civil society as well as writers, thinkers and artists. In effect Gramsci is saying that the party has the function of leading the struggles for political, moral and intellectual reform needed for the achievement of the hegemony of the working class and for the transition to socialism. But while these passages on the party are expressed in his own unique language, they do not describe the role of the party in terms which substantially differ from those used by Lenin or by Gramsci himself in the years 1923-26.

Another theme in the Prison Notebooks is the contrast between bureaucratic and democratic centralism. Thus Gramsci says that democratic centralism is 'a continual adaptation of the organisation to the real movement, a matching of thrusts from below with orders from above, a continual insertion of elements thrown up from the rank and file into the solid framework of the leadership apparatus which ensures continuity and the regular accumulation of experience'. And later in the same note he says that 'democratic centralism offers an elastic formula, which can be embodied in many diverse forms; it comes alive in so far as it is interpreted and continually adapted to necessity' (SPN 188-9). In this note, which is part of the series entitled 'The Modern Prince', Gramsci is discussing democratic centralism as a form of organisation of a state, for he refers to the French Revolution and to the unification of Italy. His remarks do not therefore directly refer to the organisation of a revolutionary party. But even if he did have political parties in mind, these remarks are fully in line with Lenin's views on the party. In particular Lenin would have agreed with the description of democratic centralism as an elastic formula, for he repeatedly stressed that the form of organisation of the Bolshevik Party was dependent on the tasks confronting the party at any particular time; what was appropriate in the conditions of illegality in the years 1900-1904, when the party had to be organised in a hierarchical and secretive fashion, became quite inappropriate in the more relaxed political atmosphere of the years 1904-7, when open party meetings were possible and the party could be built up from below on the principles of democratic elections and the autonomy of local party organisations.[34]

There is one further important passage on political parties in the Prison Notebooks: 'In the modern world, a party is such ... when it is conceived, organised and led in ways and in forms such that it will develop integrally into a state (an integral state, and not into a government technically understood) and into a conception of the world' (SPN 267). Bearing in mind Gramsci's use of the term 'integral state' to refer to the social relationships of civil society as well as those of the state, it does seem that he is thinking that a single political party could represent the working class in a socialist society.

We may conclude that Gramsci does not advance the theory of a revolutionary party beyond the stage it reached under Lenin. His thinking on the party, as on parliamentary democracy, was not brought into line with his concepts of hegemony, civil society and war of position.

Togliatti and the Italian Communist Party

A major advance in the theory and practice of a revolutionary party was made by the Italian Communist Party after the Second World War, under the creative leadership of Palmiro Togliatti who was one of the original members of the *Ordine Nuovo* group in Turin. Togliatti was a member of the Executive Committee of the Comintern from 1927 until its dissolution in 1943; he played a leading part in its Seventh Congress in 1935 and participated in the Spanish Civil War as an envoy of the Comintern. His view of the Spanish Republic was discussed in Chapter 7 in the section on war of position (p. 76). He saw it as an intermediate form of state which, had it emerged victorious, would have facilitated further transformations in the direction of socialism.

By the end of the Second World War, the moral and political prestige of the Italian Communist Party had grown enormously owing to the leading part it had played in the Resistance. It had become a mass party with over 1,700,000 members. In speeches made in 1944 Togliatti outlined the perspective for the future. It was necessary to build up the alliance between Communists, Socialists and Catholics which had come into existence during the Resistance. Italy should be transformed into a democratic, anti-fascist republic based on a plurality of political forces, which would include not only the traditional parties of the left (Socialist and Communist) but also the Christian Democratic Party which organised the Catholic workers, and especially the peasants. The aim was to transform the Italian state into what he called a 'progressive democracy' in which the working class would be the leading (hegemonic) force. The Italian road to socialism was conceived by Togliatti as a process, and as the discovery of transitional forms of advance, and he stressed that this road would be different from the insurrectionary road followed by the Bolshevik Party in 1917. The immediate aims were a democratic constitution, and measures to eliminate the social and economic roots of fascism. To carry out this strategy the Communist Party should become what Togliatti called a 'new party' (*partito nuovo*) with three main qualities:

1) It should be a 'party of government'. It should no longer be confined to criticism and propaganda, building up its strength until the time was ripe for the capture of power. This did not mean that it should necessarily take part in the government (though it did participate in the Italian Government in 1946-47). But it should continuously intervene in the life of the country, in the factories and in the villages, in a positive and constructive way.

2) The party must have a *national* character, that is, it must be a party 'which poses and solves the problems of the emancipation of labour within our national life and liberation in claiming for itself all the progressive traditions of the nation'.[35] The party should strive to be the organised expression of the working class and of all the popular strata.

3) The party should be a mass, popular party, not a small sect of highly-disciplined cadres, and should be as decentralised as possible.

The transformation of the Italian Communist Party from a party of opposition to a party of government, in the national and international conditions which have prevailed since 1944, has proved extremely difficult. The progressive democratic state, with the working class as the hegemonic force, has not yet been achieved. Nevertheless, the Italian Communist Party has established itself as a powerful political force in the life of the country. It has played a major part in building up a network of mass organisations – political, social, cooperative and cultural. Ever since Togliatti's interview with *Nuovo argomenti* after the Twentieth Congress of the CPSU in 1956, the Italian Party has been in the lead among European Communist Parties in developing a critical evaluation of the Soviet Union and other Socialist states in Eastern Europe, and in affirming that the advance to socialism consists in the expansion of democracy. In contrast to the experiences of social-democratic governments, which have not led to socialism, and to the path followed by the Soviet Union and other socialist states, the party speaks of the 'third road' to socialism, a road which is peculiarly well fitted to Western Europe with its deeply-rooted traditions of struggle for religious, cultural and political freedoms. In the mid-1970s the Italian party, in a series of joint statements with French, Spanish and other Communist parties (including the British), declared that the advance to socialism could only take place on the basis of the extension of personal and collective liberties and the plurality of political parties. These statements gave rise to the term 'Euro-communism'. But a Euro-communist strategy was not a new discovery made only in the 1970s; it was in fact the strategy of a war of position, of revolution as a process of democratic advance, which the Italian Communist Party had been following since the end of the war.

The prospects in Britain

If the 'third road' is proving difficult in Italy, what are the prospects in Britain? There are many features in our history which account for the slow development of a revolutionary movement, such as the skill, cunning and resilience of the ruling class, the absence of a revolutionary tradition persisting after the end of the Chartist movement and, since the Second World War, the polarisation between the two blocs centred on the United States and the Soviet Union. Of great importance is the deep-rooted influence of social democracy in the working class, and the special character of the Labour Party which creates both opprotunities and obstacles.

The progress made by the left inside the Labour Party since about 1978 has demonstrated the great potential which exists for its development into a more socialist and campaigning party. But the advance in the constituency parties needs to be accompanied by a corresponding advance in the political consciousness of the mass of trade union members, if the alliance with the trade unions, the fundamental source of the party's strength, is to be maintained and developed. The left needs to recognise that social democracy remains strong not only among Labour MPs, but also among six million affiliated trade unionists and many constituency party members. Bringing about a substantial development of socialist consciousness among these millions is bound to be a prolonged process. The left needs to be on guard against the temptation of advocating short cuts which could have the final effect of delaying, rather than hastening, it.

The transformation of the Labour Party from a mainly electoral party into a campaigning socialist party requires big changes in the political practice of its members. A party aiming for revolutionary social change needs to develop the ability to take political initiatives that 'weld the present to the future', that is, to find the immediate issues which link the current situation to the strategic perspective and help to shift the balance of forces in favour of the labour movement. As Gramsci said, it is 'knowing how to find each time the point of progressive equilibrium'.

The history of the Labour movement in Britain, as well as its current position, also poses the question of whether the necessary changes within the movement can be brought about in the absence of a specific organisation of Marxists – in other words the revolutionary party for which Gramsci argued. Although we may recognise that he might in the course of time have developed ideas about it beyond those of Lenin, there is, I think, no doubt that he would have maintained his conviction of the need for such a party.

By its very nature the Labour Party does not, and cannot, fulfil such a role. It includes, and should include, non-Marxists, as well as Marxists, and indeed the non-Marxists are in the great majority. Its activities and form of organisation are oriented particularly toward the electoral field, and though the left is attempting to extend the area of extra-parliamentary activity its success has so far been limited. Moreover the character of the party as a coalition of different trends and ideological outlooks is also reflected in its relatively loose forms of organisation.

Two examples illustrate the problem. In what might be called the sphere of practical political activity, the failure to maintain a daily newspaper of the Labour and trade union movement. In the sphere of theory – which also has profound repercussions in political practice – the long-standing weakness of the Labour Party (including many of its left members) in facing up to the problem of the capitalist state.

I am sure that there will be very different views among readers of this book about the way in which Marxists should react. Some will feel that they should join the Labour Party and work inside it for its transformation into a socialist party, others that they should join one of the groups influenced by the ideas of Trotsky, and others that they can best contribute without belonging to any political party, but by working as individual Marxists in the movement against nuclear weapons, the women's movement or other social movements. There will also be those who, like myself, feel that the British Communist Party is the organisation of Marxists which they should seek to strengthen, not with the objective of replacing the Labour Party by the Communist Party, but of working as an organised force in association with others to raise the socialist consciousness of the Labour and democratic movement as a whole.

Thorough consideration of all these alternatives would make this chapter excessively long and go beyond the scope of this book, which is intended only to be an introduction to Gramsci's ideas. Nevertheless, it seems to me that his ideas strengthen the case for the Communist Party.

I would suggest that the role of a revolutionary party is threefold:

1. The development of Marxist theory and the conduct of ideological struggle for intellectual and moral reform.

2. The working out of a clear strategic perspective for each stage of the advance to socialism.

3. The taking of political initiatives (based on a concrete analysis of the current situation) which will stimulate mass struggle and help to build up a bloc of social forces in line with the strategic perspective.

My own opinion is that the British Communist Party has the potentiality to do these three things, even though it has not yet developed into a major political force in Britain.

It has developed a clear strategic perspective, set out in its programme *The British Road to Socialism*, for a revolutionary strategy centred on a 'broad democratic alliance', which is a creative development in British conditions of Gramsci's concepts of hegemony and war of position. The perspective is for a 'Labour government of a new type' which would be the outcome of the broad democratic alliance and would begin to carry out a major democratic transformation of the state, and implement the left alternative economic strategy for expansion towards full employment by means of a system of democratic planning, based on an extension of public ownership and public control over monopoly capital, combined with a great expansion of industrial democracy. This would not be a socialist government, but a first stage in the transition to socialism – a stage which, if successfully achieved, would mobilise popular support for subsequent left governments which would carry out more far-reaching programmes.

The Communist Party has long experience of mass campaigning, stretching back to the 1920s. It has strong roots in the trade unions and a tradition of workplace organisation – an essential element of revolutionary practice which the Labour Party is only beginning to tackle. It has sustained a daily newspaper since 1930 and has a well-established theoretical journal in *Marxism Today*. Thus it is well placed to conduct the ideological struggle for socialism. And it is organised in such a way that it can take political initiatives within the framework of its strategic perspective.

This claim is in part founded on a characteristic which it shares with the Italian and other Communist Parties, that of being organised on the basis of democratic centralism. As Gramsci says (p. 121) this is an elastic principle which requires continual adaptation to changing conditions. If this is done, it should enable the party to intervene effectively as a united collective. Its leadership should be democratically elected and accountable to the membership, and in working out its policy it should be able to draw on a wide range of experience and opinion of a membership which is active in the workplaces and local communities as well as in the social movements making up the broad democratic alliance. For this to occur, the party must be pluralistic (not monolithic as is the Communist Party of the Soviet Union), permitting the existence of different positions or tendencies, and recognising the value of debate between them for the development of strategy and tactics, but avoiding the division of the party into organised factions which hinder united action. Thus the aim is to achieve unity in diversity within the overall strategic perspective. It may be argued that this kind of organisation, which requires an active and well-informed membership, is difficult to achieve. Nevertheless, it does seem that it is the sort of organisation required by a Marxist party which is designed to play an active, mobilising role in Britain, rather than operating as an electoral machine.

Two factors, one international and one national, have created very severe difficulties for the Communist Party in Britain. The polarisation of the world into two main blocs has clearly operated very greatly to its disadvantage. It strongly disapproved of the invasions of Czechoslovakia and Afghanistan and of the introduction of martial law in Poland in December 1981, and it has repeatedly condemned the treatement of dissidents in the Soviet Union. The strategic perspective set out in *The British Road to Socialism* is, as argued above, a creative development in British conditions of Gramsci's war of position, aiming for a transition to socialism which will be quite different from that in the Soviet Union and the other countries of exisiting socialism. Yet the Communist

Party continues to suffer because the British people, deeply influenced by the mass media, associate it with the negative aspects of the Soviet system. The way forward here can only be to continue to assert its complete autonomy as a party and its determination to build friendly relations with all communist, socialist and progressive parties throughout the world. As the Italian Communist Party has declared, the idea of a world communist movement, homogeneous and separate from the socialist and progressive parties, is now outmoded and such a movement is no longer required.

The major problem for the Communist Party, which has confronted it ever since its foundation in 1920, is that of its relationship to the Labour Party. The deep-rooted influence of reformist and social democratic ideas in the British Labour movement has meant that the right wing has always enjoyed substantial support. Moreover, the unique character of the Labour Party (discussed on p. 106) as the political representative of the trade union movement, has had two consequences for the Communist Party. On the one hand, it means that individual Communists can play some part in Labour Party affairs as political-levy-paying members of affiliated trade unions. On the other hand, it gives rise to a deep loyalty to the Labour Party among many trade union members, leading them to give their electoral support to it rather than the Communist Party, though within the unions they often elect Communists to leading positions.

There have been exceptions, such as the election of Gallacher as an MP in 1935, and of Gallacher and Piratin in 1945, but these arose out of special circumstances. The only period when the loyalty of trade unionists to the Labour Party did not operate against the Communist Party was in the early 1920s. Although the Communist Party's application for affiliation to the Labour Party (made immediately after its founding conference) was turned down, Communist Party members were able to remain in the Labour Party as individual members and be adopted as Labour candidates. For example, in the general election of 1922 the Communist S. Saklatvala was adopted as official Labour Party candidate in

Battersea North, and was elected to parliament. Affiliated trade unions were also able to elect communists as delegates to Labour Party conferences and Harry Pollitt, for example, attended the annual Labour Party conference as a delegate from the Boilermakers' Society up to 1927. However, between 1925 and 1928, resolutions were passed at annual Labour Party conferences excluding communists from individual membership of the party, and preventing trade unions from sending communists as delegates to party conferences. Ever since then, the anomalous position has existed, that communists who pay the political levy as trade unionists are affiliated trade union members of the Labour Party but are deprived of the right to act as delegates to its conferences.

The Labour Party came into existence in 1899 in the form of the Labour Representation Committee, not only to represent the trade unions in parliament, but also as an alliance between the trade unions and socialist parties, principally the Independent Labour Party but including the Social Democratic Federation, the small Marxist party which disaffiliated in 1902, but affiliated again in 1916 as the British Socialist Party. The latter was one of the main components of the Communist Party when it was founded in 1920. Thus the Labour Party had a federal character, designed to unite all the different trends in the labour movement. After the Communist Party's first application for affiliation was turned down, a further six applications were made on various occasions up to 1946. The highest vote ever recorded for affiliation was in June 1943 – 712,000 (nearly 27 per cent) in favour and 1,951,000 against. The last application was defeated in 1946. Since then the Communist Party has not campaigned for affiliation, but has concentrated on the removal of bans and proscriptions and especially on the restoration of the right of trade unionists to elect whomever they wish, from among their members paying the political levy, to represent them as delegates to Labour Party conferences. The 1978 edition of the *British Road to Socialism* says that if the bans and proscriptions were removed, new opportunities will open up for still more developed forms of Labour-Communist unity, including the possibility of affiliation to the Labour Party.

I think it can be justifiably maintained that this brief survey of a long and complex relationship shows that, as the left in the Labour Party grows stronger, a way could be found for establishing much closer links with the Communist Party. These links would greatly help to strengthen the Labour Party left, counteracting the damaging influence of the Militant Tendency and other leftist tendencies.

The forging of left unity – an alliance between the Labour Party left, the Communist Party and like-minded people in other parties and social movements – would create a dynamism leading towards the building of a new historic bloc in Britain. But for this to occur, a much wider understanding and further development of the Marxist theory of politics, enriched by the ideas of Antonio Gramsci, is a necessity.

Notes

References to Gramsci's works in the text are abbreviated as follows:

Selections from the Prison Notebooks, edited and translated by Quintin Hoare and Geoffrey Nowell Smith, Lawrence and Wishart, London, 1971.   SPN

Selections from Political Writings, 1910-20, selected and edited by Quintin Hoare, translated by John Mathews, Lawrence and Wishart, London, 1977.   SPW I

Selections from Political Writings, 1921-26, translated and edited by Quintin Hoare, Lawrence and Wishart, London, 1978.   SPW II

Quaderni del Carcere, edited by Valentino Gerratana, Einaudi, Torino, 1975. The complete critical edition of the Prison Notebooks, prepared by the Gramsci Institute in Rome, in three volumes with a fourth volume containing notes, index, etc., edited and with a preface by V. Gerratana.   Q

Chapter 1

1. Lenin, *Collected Works*, Vol. 17, pp. 57-8.

2. The limitations of Leninism are discussed in the article by Ernesto Laclau and Chantal Mouffe entitled 'Socialist Strategy. Where Next?' in *Marxism Today*, January 1981. What I have written in this chapter and elsewhere in this book owes a great deal to their outstanding pioneering work on Gramsci. The ideas in their article are elaborated at greater length in their forthcoming book *Hegemony and Socialist Strategy*.

3. The nature of social democracy is discussed on pages 53

and 106.

4. George Matthews, *The Communist Party, 1920-80*, CPGB, 1980, p. 8.

5. *Antonio Gramsci. Life of a Revolutionary* translated by Tom Nairn, NLB, London, 1970.

Chapter 2

6. *New Left Review*, 100, November 1976-January 1977, pp. 15-17 in an article entitled 'The Antinomies of Antonio Gramsci'.

7. This is the revised version of this passage. When Gramsci was rewriting some of his notes after 1931 he tended to replace the term 'class' by 'social group' presumably to avoid arousing the suspicions of the prison censor. However the term social group has a certain advantage for it can be understood to refer, not only to a class, but to part of a class or a particular category of the population. When Gramsci wishes to refer to one of the major social classes (bourgeoisie or proletariat) he uses the phrase 'fundamental social group'.

Chapter 3

8. *Lenin's Political Thought*, Vol I, *Theory and Practice in the Democratic Revolution*, Macmillan, 1977, p. 107.

9. Gramsci derived this motto from the French writer Romain Rolland.

Chapter 4

10. Earlier analyses were made in the theses presented by Gramsci and Togliatti to the Third Congress of the Italian Communist Party held at Lyons in January 1926 (SPW II 340) and in the unfinished article 'Some aspects of the Southern Question' (SPW II 441) which Gramsci was writing at the time of his arrest.

Chapter 5

11. See, for example, the essays by Bob Jessop and Stuart Hall in *Marxism and Democracy*, edited by Alan Hunt

(Lawrence and Wishart, 1980), and *Silver Linings*, edited by George Bridges and Rosalind Brunt (Lawrence and Wishart, 1981), especially 'Popular Politics and Marxist Theory in Britain' by Bill Schwarz and Colin Mercer.

12. This suggestion is made by Robert Gray in his article 'Political Ideology and Class Struggle under Early Industrial Capitalism' in *Marxism Today*, December 1977, p. 370.

13. Ernesto Laclau and Chantal Mouffe 'Socialist Strategy Where Next?', in *Marxism Today*, January 1981, p. 21.

14. *Politics and Ideology in Marxist Theory*, NLB, 1977.

15. Gramsci also uses the term 'national-popular' when he compares Italian with French literature and contends that the Italians had no national-popular literature comparable with the popular French novels written in the nineteenth century (Q 2113-20). He also says that French culture had a more strictly national-popular character in that the intellectuals, because of certain specific traditions, tended more than elsewhere to approach the people in order to guide them ideologically and keep them linked with the ruling group (SPN 421). At this point the editors of the SPN insert a note, to the effect that the notion of national-popular is perhaps best taken as describing a sort of 'historic bloc' between national and popular aspirations in the formation of which the intellectuals play an essential mediating role, and that it is a 'cultural concept'. This misses the essential features of Gramsci's 'national-popular collective will' as the combination of popular-democratic aspirations with the class objectives of the hegemonic class (a political-ideological concept rather than a cultural one) and is perhaps one of the very few of the editors' perceptive notes which misunderstand one of Gramsci's concepts.

Chapter 6

16. Gramsci also uses the term 'passive revolution' in a different, though related sense, to denote the way in which the capitalist class rose to ascendancy in Italy, Germany and

other countries through a process of gradual, molecular change in the course of which the old feudal classes were transformed, in contrast to the French Revolution when they were overthrown: 'the demands which in France found a Jacobin-Napoleonic expression were satisfied by small doses, legally, in a reformist manner – in such a way that it was possible to preserve the political and economic position of the old feudal classes, to avoid agrarian reform and, especially, to avoid the popular masses going through a period of political experience such as occurred in France in the years of Jacobinism' (SPN 119) and see Anne Sassoon, *Gramsci's Politics*, Croom Helm, 1980, pp. 204-10.

Chapter 7

17. *Marxism Today*, October 1978, p. 314. This brief analysis of mid-Victorian society has also drawn on Robert Gray's article 'Politics, Ideology and Class struggle under early industrial capitalism' in *Marxism Today*, December 1977.

18. Thatcherism is examined by Stuart Hall in his essay 'Popular-democratic vs authoritarian populism' in *Marxism and Democracy*, edited by Alan Hunt (1980) and by Andrew Gamble in his essay 'The free economy and the strong state' in *Socialist Register, 1979* and his article 'The decline of the Conservative Party' in *Marxism Today*, November 1979.

Chapter 8

19. This chapter leans to a great extent on Chantal Mouffe's essay 'Hegemony and Ideology in Gramsci' in the volume of essays edited by her, *Gramsci and Marxist Theory*, RKP, 1979. In this essay, which makes a most valuable interpretation of Gramsci's concept of ideology, she also considered the relation between Gramsci's approach and Althusser's theory of ideology as a 'lived relation' between people and their world.

20. *Letters from Prison* by Antonio Gramsci, selected, translated and edited by Lynne Lawner, Jonathan Cape, 1975, p. 193.

21. Palmiro Togliatti, *On Gramsci and Other Writings* edited

and introduced by Donald Sassoon, Lawrence and Wishart, 1979, p. 145.

22. Regrettably, these notes are not yet available in English, though a few of the most important passages are quoted in footnotes in the SPN, e.g. pp. 55-6.

23. James Joll, *Gramsci*, Fontana Modern Masters, Collins, 1977, p. 112.

Chapter 9

24. For a useful discussion of Foucault, see Colin Mercer's essay 'Revolutions, reforms or reformulations? Marxist discourse on democracy' in *Marxism and Democracy,* edited by Alan Hunt, Lawrence and Wishart, 1980, pp. 122-23.

24a. G. Dimitrov, *The Working Class against Fascism. Report of 2 August 1935, Seventh Congress of the Communist International,* pp. 58-64.

24b. Speech made at the discussion on September 18-19, 1936 at the secretariat of the Executive Committee of the Comintern, *Outline History of the Communist International,* Moscow, 1971, p. 416.

24c. *It Can be Done,* Report of the 1937 Congress of the Communist Party.

24d. Donald Sassoon, *The Strategy of the Italian Communist Party,* Frances Pinter, 1981, p. 13.

Chapter 11

25. In his essay 'Power and Participation' Richard Gunn examines the work of Habermas and other writers of the Frankfurt School in developing the concept of a 'political public sphere', which is restricted and distorted under capitalism. From this, Gunn draws a distinction between politics as power and politics as participation; in the transition to communism politics as power dies away while politics as participation grows with the continual expansion of the political public sphere. This corresponds with Gramsci's perspective of the transformation and extension of civil society. The relation between Habermas's political public sphere and Gramsci's civil society deserves to be further explored. Gunn

also argues that Marx's concept of *praxis* contains the germ of this approach. The essay is in *Class, Hegemony and Party*, edited by Jon Bloomfield, Lawrence and Wishart, 1977. It is relevant to note that Gramsci used the term 'philosophy of praxis' for Marxism in his Prison Notebooks.

Chapter 12

26. Letter to Tatiana of 19 March 1927. *Letters from Prison* by Antonio Gramsci, selected, translated and edited by Lynne Lawner, Jonathan Cape, 1975, p. 79.

27. This account of Sorel's views and of Gramsci's relations with Sorel is taken from Christine Buci-Glucksmann, *Gramsci and the State*, Lawrence and Wishart, 1980 pp. 66-8.

28. The relation between intellectuals and the labour movement is considered by Eric Hobsbawm in *Marxism Today*, July 1979; his account begins with some comments on Gramsci's views.

29. Palmiro Togliatti *On Gramsci and Other Writings*, edited and introduced by Donald Sassoon, Lawrence and Wishart, 1979, pp. 155 and 177.

30. The English translation of this and the above passage is taken from *Gramsci* by James Joll, Fontana, 1977, p. 101.

Chapter 13

31. The next two sections of this chapter owe a great deal to the last chapter of *The Road from Thatcherism. The Alernative Economic Strategy* by Sam Aaronovitch, Lawrence and Wishart, 1981.

32. For the full story of the Poplar battles, see *Poplarism* by Noreen Branson, Lawrence and Wishart, 1979.

33. Article by Keith Dixon and Daniel Perraud on France in *Marxism Today*, September 1981.

34. Lenin, 'The Reorganisation of the Party' (November 1905), *Collected Works*, Vol. 10 p. 314, and Neil Harding, *Lenin's Political Thought*, Macmillan, 1977, p. 231.

35. P. Togliatti, 'Che cosa e il partito nuovo?' in *Rinascita*, No. 4, Oct-Nov-Dec. 1944. This section on the Italian Communist Party is largely based on the analysis by Donald

Sassoon in *The Strategy of the Italian Communist Party*, Frances Pinter, 1981 and his introduction to Togliatti's *On Gramsci and Other Writings*, Lawrence and Wishart, 1979.

Chronology of Gramsci's Life

1891 January 22. Born at Ales in the province of Cagliari, Sardinia. Fourth son of Francesco Gramsci, a clerk in the local registrar's office at Ghilarza, and Giuseppina Marcias.

1897-98 His father is sentenced to five years' imprisonment on charges of maladministration. On his release he has no job, so Antonio Gramsci and his six brothers and sisters grow up in difficult circumstances and deep financial insecurity. Gramsci suffered ill health throughout his life, and from a deformity which left him a hunchback.

1903 On completing his elementary education, has to leave school and work for two years in the local registry office in Ghilarza where the family moved after his father's imprisonment.

1905 Education resumed at Santa Lussurgiu and then at Cagliari.

1911 Wins a scholarship at Turin University and begins his studies there; another successful candidate was Palmiro Togliatti. In his first year studies linguistics, Italian literature, geography, Latin and Greek grammar; in later years, moral philosophy, modern history and Greek literature.

1913 Participates in Sardinia in the first elections held on the basis of universal suffrage, and makes his first contacts with the socialist movement in Turin.

1914 Writes his first article for the Socialist paper *Il Grido del Popolo.*

1916 Begins work as a journalist for the Socialist Party paper

Avanti!, writing theatrical reviews and contributing a polemical column. Writes also for *Il Grido del Popolo*.

1917 Takes part in the preparations to welcome delegates from the Russian soviets. After the four-day spontaneous insurrection of the Turin workers in August and the arrest of most of the Socialist leaders, Gramsci is elected to the Provisional Committee of the Socialist Party. On 24 December celebrates the Russian Revolution with the article 'The Revolution against *Capital*' in *Avanti!*

1919 May. Founds the weekly journal *L'Ordine Nuovo* with his friends Togliatti, Tasca and Terracini. In June writes the article 'Workers' Democracy' proposing that the 'Internal Commissions' should be transformed into factory councils as 'organs of proletarian power'. *L'Ordine Nuovo* becomes the organ of the factory councils in Turin.

1920 April. General strike in Turin and Piedmont in defence of the factory councils ends in a partial victory for the employers, owing to the refusal of the leadership of the Socialist Party and the trade unions to extend it beyond Piedmont.

September. Participates in the month-long occupation of the factories which spreads from Milan throughout Italy.

1921 January. Attends the Leghorn congress of the Italian Socialist Party at which the party splits and the Italian Communist Party is founded. Gramsci is elected to the central committee. However the principal influence in the party is not that of the *L'Ordine Nuovo* group with its concern for the factory councils and the relations between the party and the masses, but that of its general secretary Amadeo Bordiga with his stress on discipline and centralism, and purity of principles. Gramsci remains in Turin as editor of *L'Ordine Nuovo*, now a daily paper.

1922 May. Arrives in Moscow as member of the Executive of the Communist International (Comintern).

Spends some months in a clinic near Moscow where he meets his future wife Giulia Schucht.

October 28. The 'March on Rome'; Mussolini's fascists seize power in Italy.

November-December. Takes part in the Fourth Congress of the Comintern.

1923 While Gramsci is still in Moscow, the police arrest many leading members of the Italian Communist Party, including Bordiga.

November. Moves to Vienna, where he engages in a correspondence with Togliatti, Terracini and others discussing the new strategy he proposes for the party.

1924 April. Elected deputy in the Veneto constituency.

May. Returns to Italy as leader of Communist Party.

June. Assassination of the Socialist deputy Matteotti. Participates in the secession of the parliamentary opposition to the Aventine while campaigning against its passivity and legalism. In November the Communist deputies return to the Chamber.

1925 May. Makes a speech in the Chamber of Deputies against Mussolini's proposal for a law banning all secret associations including the Freemasons.

1926 January. Takes part in the Third Congress of the Italian Communist Party at Lyons in France. The congress approves the 'Lyons Theses' drafted by Gramsci and Togliatti by an overwhelming majority, confirming that the leftist influence previously exerted by Bordiga has been largely overcome.

October. Writes to the Central Committee of the Communist Party of the Soviet Union expressing the Italian Party's fears that the fierceness of the struggle between Stalin and Trotsky could end by destroying the leading function which the CPSU had won through Lenin's contribution.

November 8. Arrested in Rome. Sent to a camp for political prisoners on the island of Ustica. His friend Piero Sraffa (living in England) arranges for him to receive books.

1927 January. Transferred to prison in Milan.

March. In a letter to his sister-in-law Tatiana says he is plagued by the idea of accomplishing something *für ewig* (for ever). Sets out systematic plan of study. He had thought of four subjects: the history of Italian intellectuals, comparative linguistics, the drama of Pirandello, and popular literature. However, his request for permission to write is refused.

1928 May. Transferred to prison in Rome.

June. Condemned to 20 years' imprisonment. Sent to the Special Penal Prison at Turi, near Bari.

1929 January. Receives permission to write.

February 8. Date of the first 'Prison Notebook'.

March. Tells Tatiana in a letter he has decided on three main subjects: the history of Italy in the nineteenth century with special regard to the formation and development of groups of intellectuals; the theory of history and of historiography; Americanism and Fordism.

1930 November-December. Begins a series of discussions with other communists in the prison on various themes including a constituent assembly. In 1928-29 the Comintern had abandoned its strategy of the united front, describing social democrats as 'social fascists', and envisaging the overthrow of fascism by a socialist revolution. Gramsci, on the other hand, foresaw an intermediate democratic phase and put forward the slogan of a 'constituent assembly'. The Italian Communist Party had adopted the Comintern view. Gramsci's approach aroused sharp differences among the prisoners, and he suspended the discussions.

1931 August. Suffers a serious haemorrhage.

1933 March. Further serious illness. After medical examination and an international campaign organised by Piero Sraffa and supported by, among others, Romain Rolland and Henri Barbusse, is transferred in December to a clinic at Formia.

1935 August. Transferred to the Cusumano Clinic in Rome. His mind remains lucid, but he is too ill to continue working on his notebooks.

1937 April 27. Dies after a cerebral haemorrhage. Tatiana manages to smuggle the thirty-three notebooks out of Gramsci's room and via the diplomatic bag to Moscow.

1947 A first collection of Gramsci's letters from prison (with many cuts) published.

1948-51 Publication of the Prison Notebooks in six volumes.

1965 Complete edition of Gramsci's letters published, edited by Sergio Caprioglio and Elsa Fubini.

1971 Publication in Britain of *Selections from the Prison Notebooks*.

1975 Publication of the complete edition of the Prison Notebooks in four volumes, edited by Valentino Gerratana.

Bibliography

Gramsci's writings – English translations of Gramsci's writings are listed at the beginning of the Notes. The *Selections from the Prison Notebooks* has a very good introduction giving the historical background to the main events in Gramsci's life. In addition there is:

> *Letters from Prison*, Lynne Lawner, London, Jonathan Cape, 1975. This includes 94 letters, well annotated, out of the total of 428 in the Einaudi edition of 1965.

The following is a selection of works on Gramsci in English.

Anderson, Perry, 'The Antinomies of Antonio Gramsci', *New Left Review*, No. 100, Nov. 1976-Jan. 1977.
> A criticism of Gramsci and of his strategy of war of position, from a Trotskyist viewpoint. Concludes that 'in the labyrinth of the Notebooks, Gramsci lost his way'.

Boggs, Carl, *Gramsci's Marxism*, Pluto Press, 1976.
> The first short introduction in English to Gramsci's political thought. Suffers from a tendency to identify hegemony with ideological domination, and from a complete misunderstanding of Lenin.

Buci-Glucksmann, Christine, *Gramsci and the State*, Lawrence and Wishart, 1980.
> A formidable work of great scholarship, providing a great deal of information about and analysis of the Prison Notebooks, relating them to the historical context in which they were written. Directs attention particularly to Gramsci's theory of the state, and is very instructive on

Gramsci's relations with Lenin, and also with Bukharin.

Cammett, John M., *Antonio Gramsci and the Origins of Italian Communism*, California, Stanford University Press, 1967.
A pioneering study of Gramsci's life and ideas combined with a history of the Italian labour movement before, during and after the First World War.

Clark, Martin, *Antonio Gramsci and the Revolution that Failed*, Yale University Press, 1977.
A discussion of the background to Gramsci's political activities in the factory councils' movement in Turin and in the foundation of the Italian Communist Party in 1921.

Davidson, Alistair, *Antonio Gramsci. Towards an Intellectual Biography*, Merlin Press, 1977.
A sensitive account of Gramsci's life and intellectual development, especially of his childhood in Sardinia and his life in Turin.

Davidson, Alistair, *The Theory and Practice of Italian Communism*, Vol. I, Merlin Press, 1982.
The first volume of a longer study of the theory and practice of Italian Communism, starting with the foundation of the Italian Socialist Party in 1892 and going up to 1940.

David, John A. (ed.), *Gramsci and Italy's Passive Revolution*, Croom Helm, 1979.
A collection of essays on Italian history in the nineteenth century, discussing passive revolution and other themes in Gramsci's Prison Notebooks.

Entwistle, Harold. *Antonio Gramsci: Conservative Schooling for Radical Politics*, Routledge & Kegan Paul, 1979.
The first study in English of Gramsci's ideas about education.

Femia, Joseph V., *Gramsci's Political Thought. Hegemony, Consciousness and the Revolutionary Process*, Oxford University Press, 1981.
A scholarly, wide-ranging and perceptive study of Gramsci's concept of hegemony understood as ideological ascendancy.

Fiori, Giuseppe, *Antonio Gramsci*, New Left Books, 1970.
The best Italian biography of Gramsci, translated by Tom Nairn.

Hall, Stuart, Bob Lumley and Gregor McLennan, 'Politics and ideology in Gramsci, in *Cultural Studies 10* edited by Gregor McLennan, Birmingham Centre for Cultural Studies, 1977.
A study of Gramsci's theory of ideology, and the use made of it by Althusser and Poulantzas.

Joll, James, *Gramsci*, Fontana Modern Masters, Collins, 1977.
A very good short account of Gramsci's life and ideas.

Laclau, Ernesto, 'Fascism and Ideology' in *Politics and Ideology in Marxist Theory*, NLB, 1977.
Arguably the most important contribution to the concept of hegemony made by any non-Italian Marxist.

Mercer, Colin, 'Revolutions, Reforms or Reformulations? Marxist Discourse on Democracy' in *Marxism and Democracy* edited by Alan Hunt, Lawrence and Wishart, 1980.
Considers the principal elements in Gramsci's concept of hegemony in a very illuminating way.

Mouffe, Chantal (ed.), *Gramsci and Marxist Theory*, Routledge and Kegan Paul, 1979.
A collection of essays on Gramsci mainly by Italian writers, but including one by the editor on 'Hegemony and Ideology in Gramsci' which is a valuable contribution to understanding Gramsci's theory of ideology.

Sassoon, Anne Showstack, *Gramsci's Politics*, Croom Helm, 1980.
Beginning with his earliest writings and extending to the Prison Notebooks, examines Gramsci's writings on politics, the political party, the state and the revolutionary process, thus providing a valuable account of the evolution of his ideas.

Sassoon, Anne Showstack (ed.), *Approaches to Gramsci*, Writers and Readers, 1982.
A collection of articles by Italian, French and English authors (including two by the editor) throwing new light on his political thought, and including a discussion of his observations on folklore.

Sassoon, Donald, *The Strategy of the Italian Communist Party. From the Resistance to the Historic Compromise*, Frances Pinter,

1982.

A study of the postwar strategy of the Italian Communist Party and of the difficulties it has faced in translating this strategy into practice. Indispensable for an understanding of Euro-communism.

Spriano, Paolo, *Antonio Gramsci and the Party. The Prison Years*, Lawrence and Wishart, 1979.

The author of the five-volume history of the Italian Communist Party sets out all that is known about Gramsci's political and personal relations with the Italian Communist Party during his years in prison.

Togliatti, Palmiro, *Gramsci and Other Writings*, Lawrence and Wishart, 1979.

A selection of Togliatti's writings from 1925, including the account of the formation of the new leading group in the Italian Communist Party in 1923-34 when Gramsci became the party leader, and two articles on Gramsci.

Urry, John, *The Anatomy of Capitalist Societies. The Economy, Civil Society and the State*, Macmillan, 1981.

The first book devoted to analysing and developing Gramsci's concept of civil society.

Williams, Gwyn, *Proletarian Order. Antonio Gramsci, Factory Councils and the Origins of Italian Communism 1911-21*, Pluto Press, 1975.

A vivid study of the crisis of Italian Socialism 1911-21, focusing on Gramsci and the factory councils' movement of 1912-20 in Turin, and on the foundation of the Italian Communist Party.

Index

Index

Action Party 46-7
alternative economic strategy 88, 107
Anderson, Perry 21
anti-passive revolution 49, 78

Bordiga, Amadeo 19, 118-19
bourgeois-democratic revolution 22

Caesarism 40-1
Campbell, J.R. 76
Chartism 43, 50
civil society 67-79; defined 26, 69; in Tsarist Russia 28, 74; as fortresses and earthworks 27, 74; in transition to communism 77-8; and relations of production 85; extending sphere of politics 89-92; intellectuals and 96
class reductionism 67
class struggle 29, 69
Comintern 15-16, 75
common sense 25, 63-4
Communism 77-8
Communist Party, Chinese 43, 62
Communist Party, French 113

Communist Party of Great Britain: in 1920s and 1930s 16; *The British Road to Socialism* 17-18, 73; 1937 congress 76; traditional leftism in 113; the case for 126-31
Communist Party, Italian: Gramsci and 18-19, 35; foundation 81; Togliatti and 122-24; and world communist movement 129
Communist Party of the Soviet Union 78, 82, 124, 128
Conservative Party 41, 44, 53, 54-7
corporate: economic-corporate 23, 29-30; 'corporatism' 52
crisis, organic 37-8, 50-7
Croce, B. 65-6, 98

democracy: direct 81-2, 109; parliamentary 82, 112, 114-16; new conception of 103-4
democratic centralism 121, 128
dictatorship of the proletariat 17, 35, 82
Dimitrov, G. 16, 75-6